ANALYZING DEMAND BEHAVIOR

ANALYZING DEMAND BEHAVIOR

A Study of Energy Elasticities

DOUGLAS R. BOHI

Published for Resources for the Future, Inc.
By The Johns Hopkins University Press
Baltimore and London

Published for Resources for the Future
By The Johns Hopkins University Press, Baltimore, Maryland 21218

Library of Congress Cataloging in Publication Data

Bohi, Douglas R.
  Analyzing demand behavior.

  Includes index.
  1. Energy consumption—Mathematical models. 2. Power resources—Prices—Mathematical models. 3. Elasticity (Economics)—Mathematical models.
I. Resources for the Future. II. Title.
HD9502.A2B65   333.79′12′0724   81-47616
ISBN 0-8018-2705-1   ACR2

RESOURCES FOR THE FUTURE, INC.
1755 Massachusetts Avenue, N.W., Washington, D.C 20036

Resources for the Future is a nonprofit organization for research and education in the development, conservation, and use of natural resources and the improvement of the quality of the environment. It was established in 1952 with the cooperation of the Ford Foundation. Grants for research are accepted from government and private sources only if they meet the conditions of a policy established by the Board of Directors of Resources for the Future. The policy states that RFF shall be solely responsible for the conduct of the research and free to make the research results available to the public. Part of the work of Resources for the Future is carried out by its resident staff; part is supported by grants to universities and other nonprofit organizations. Unless otherwise stated, interpretations and conclusions in RFF publications are those of the authors; the organization takes responsibility for the selection of significant subjects for study, the competence of the researchers, and their freedom of inquiry.

This book was prepared in RFF's Center for Energy Policy Research, Milton Russell, director, and funded by the Electric Power Research Institute and Resources for the Future. Douglas R. Bohi is a senior fellow at Resources for the Future. The book was edited by Ruth Haas and designed by Elsa Williams.

Contents

Foreword

Acknowledgments

1 Introduction   1

2 Estimating the Demand for Energy:
Issues and Methodologies   7
    The Concept of Demand   7
        Individual Demand Functions   8,   *Market Demand Functions*   11,   *Definitions of Elasticities*   12
    Dynamics of Demand for Energy Products   14
        Reduced-Form Fuel Consumption Models   15,   *Structural Demand Models* 23,   *Comparing Model Specifications*   27
    Aggregation and Measurement Problems   28
    The Identification Problem   33
        Interdependence of Fuel Prices and Quantities   35,   *The Supply of Fuel-Using Equipment*   41,   *Disequilibrium Markets*   43
    Functional Forms and Related Estimation Problems   43
    Separating Influences Acting on Demand   52
    Concluding Remark   53

3 Demand for Electricity   55

Residential Electricity Demand   55
Reduced-Form Models   61,   *Structural Demand Models*   74, *Conclusions on Residential Demand for Electricity*   77
Commercial Demand for Electricity   79
Industrial Demand for Electricity   82
Aggregate Industrial Demand   83,   *Demand by Industrial Categories*   85,   *Conclusions on Industrial Demand*   90

4 Demand for Natural Gas   92

Residential and Commercial Gas Demand   93
Static Consumption Models   96,   *Dynamic Consumption Models*   100,   *Fuel Shares Models*   103,   *Structural Models*   104,   *Conclusions on Residential and Commercial Gas Demand*   105
Industrial Demand for Natural Gas   105
Manufacturing Demand for Natural Gas   107,   *Fuel Substitution in Electric Power Generation*   109,   *Conclusions on Industrial Demand*   113

5 Demand for Petroleum Products   114

Transportation Demand   114
Gasoline Demand   116,   *Conclusions on Gasoline Demand*   126,   *Other Transportation Fuels*   127
Residential and Commercial Demand for Fuel Oil   128
Industrial Demand for Fuel Oil   131

6 Demand for Coal   135

Problems of Estimating Coal Demand   136
Demand for Coal by Electric Utilities   140
Demand for Coal in Manufacturing   142
Conclusion   144

7 Summary and Conclusions   146

Estimation Problems   146
Capturing the Dynamics of Demand   147,   *Determining the Level of Aggregation*   149,   *Separating the Determinants of Demand*   151,   *Separating Supply and Demand Effects*   153, *Estimation Form and Method*   155
Measures of Price Elasticities   156
Electricity   158,   *Natural Gas*   158,   *Gasoline*   160,

Fuel Oil 160, *Coal* 161
Caveat Emptor 161
The Data 162, *The Concept* 162, *The Application* 163

References   165

Index   173

Tables

3-1 Summary of Estimated Price and Income Elasticities of Residential Demand for Electricity by Type of Model and Data   57

3-2 Summary of Estimated Price and Income Elasticities of Commercial Demand for Electricity   80

3-3 Summary of Aggregate Price and Income Elasticities of Industrial Demand for Electricity   84

3-4 Comparison of Price Elasticity Estimates by Industrial Categories   86

4-1 Summary of Estimated Price and Income Elasticities of Residential and Commercial Demand for Natural Gas   94

4-2 Summary of Own-Price and Cross-Price Elasticities of Demand for Natural Gas in Manufacturing and Electric Utilities   108

5-1 Summary of Price and Income Elasticities of Demand for Gasoline   117

5-2 Estimates of Long-Run Price and Income Elasticities of Demand for Transportation Fuels Other than Gasoline   127

5-3 Summary of Price and Income Elasticities of Residential and Commercial Demand for Fuel Oil   130

5-4 Summary of Own-Price and Cross-Price Elasticities of Demand for Fuel Oil by Manufacturing and Electric Utilities   132

6-1 Summary of Estimated Price Elasticities of Demand for Coal by Electric Utilities   141

6-2 Summary of Estimated Price Elasticities of Demand for Coal in Manufacturing   143

7-1 Summary of Information on Price Elasticities of Demand by Fuel and Sector   159

Foreword

Consumer responses to the energy price increases of the 1970s convinced the general public of what economists had long preached: "Price matters." However, neither economists nor the public have been very satisfied with the answers to the more difficult question: "But by how much?" In the case of energy, no conclusive answer is yet possible, but the numerous studies that investigate demand elasticities do offer a basis for understanding better the process of estimating demand.

Analyzing Demand Behavior: A Study of Energy Elasticities takes econometric studies as data; it examines their assumptions, investigates their methodologies, contrasts the data sets they use, and compares their results. In the end, the limitations and the promise of econometric demand analysis are illuminated for those who use them—decision makers in government and industry. At the same time, pitfalls, sources of error in interpretation, and advantages and disadvantages of alternative procedures are laid out for demand estimators themselves.

By examining an array of studies dealing with the same or related phenomena, the author is able to sort out the ways in which decisions made by researchers affect their results. This is important when demand studies are used as a guide for policy. This analysis demonstrates that estimates can be substantially different, depending on the choices the researcher makes among alternative statistical models, types of data, and estimation methods.

Because the studies examined here were about consumer response to energy prices, the reader also learns a great deal about energy demand—disaggregated by fuel and by consuming sector. Hence, this book can be of immediate use in understanding the likely effects of such policies as decontrol of natural gas, restrictions on oil imports, or marginal cost pricing of electricity. Numerical demand estimates can be compared and some of the differences among them explained. Even though these specific estimates may become dated with shifts in the economy and in energy use patterns, the insights provided are essentially timeless; they can be used in interpreting new studies as they come along.

More important, though, this book will advance the practice of demand estimation generally. By informing users what they can and cannot expect from researchers, it can sharpen the criteria that are used to commission such studies and judge their results. By alerting researchers to some special problems of estimation, it can help them avoid pitfalls and blind alleys; these can be especially serious when rapid changes are taking place in the economy. And by offering a careful critique of the state of the art, it can provide guidance for students and analysts new to demand estimation.

Analyzing Demand Behavior offers no new estimates of demand elasticities for energy. Nor does it provide a detailed description of the different studies examined; for that the reader is directed to the studies themselves. What this work does offer is the considered judgment of its author as to what wisdom can be inferred about the role of econometric demand estimation in formulating policy and understanding demand behavior.

March 1981   Milton Russell, *Director*
                                    Center for Energy Policy Research

Acknowledgments

This study is based on research performed under a grant to Resources for the Future from the Electric Power Research Institute. Its goal was a comprehensive survey of the econometric literature on energy demand elasticities and an evaluation of the reliability of the estimates for forecasting purposes. In the process of completing that work, I became increasingly aware of widespread misunderstandings about what has been accomplished in the literature and about what econometric tools can be expected to achieve. This volume addresses some of these misunderstandings by paying less attention to details in the literature and by emphasizing the connections among the problems of demand analysis, the approaches used, the estimates obtained, and the interpretation of results. Although the subject matter is energy, the same problems of estimation and application arise in connection with demand for virtually any commodity. Also, while the studies referred to here cover a period up to the beginning of 1980, and specific results will become dated with new information and research, the issues addressed will continue to persist and should be understood by practitioners and policy makers alike.

I would like to thank Albert Halter and James Eyssell of the Electric Power Research Institute for their assistance with the work on the original research grant, and Nancy Olewiler for her extensive comments on that version. V. Kerry Smith and Michael Toman read early drafts of parts of that manuscript and offered helpful suggestions.

For this work, I am indebted to Edward Erickson, Robert Halvorsen, and Raymond Kopp for their comments. I am most appreciative of the advice and comments of Milton Russell, who guided this manuscript through several drafts to its present form. I am of course solely responsible for any deficiencies that remain, some of which no doubt exist because I did not sufficiently heed the advice given.

This manuscript has also benefited from the help of Anne Farr, who tirelessly and efficiently typed many drafts; Shelley Matsuba, who had the laborious job of checking facts and references; and Ruth Haas, who edited the manuscript with her usual care and patience.

March 1981   D. R. B.

chapter 1
Introduction

A price elasticity of demand is a convenient way of summarizing how changes in market price or quantity consumed affect each other. It is the ratio of two percentages—the change in quantity consumed that results from a change in price, or vice versa. A reliable measure of this relationship would be valuable in a wide variety of applications involving pricing decisions. For example, accurate information about elasticities of demand for energy products would make it possible to answer many energy policy questions. The effectiveness of an excise tax in reducing gasoline consumption, or the impact of a reduction in oil imports on the domestic price of crude oil would become readily apparent. The fact that there are no confident answers to such questions is an indication of the nature of available information on demand elasticities. This is true for all demand elasticities, not just energy. Furthermore, in view of the comparatively large body of research that exists for energy demand, the absence of satisfactory information raises doubts about the effectiveness of econometric methods in providing reliable answers.

A cursory review of empirical studies of energy demand shows a startling lack of consensus on price elasticities. The estimates vary considerably from one study to the next, in one case suggesting that price is very important and in the next that it is not; sometimes implying that income is the controlling factor while other times suggesting price is dominant; or sometimes indicating that interfuel substitution is important and other times that it is not. If policy makers turn to research in this area for guidance, they will be confronted with a range of numbers that is frequently so wide it offers little direction. These disparities can affect the enthusiasm for a given analytical position, or they can be used to support widely disparate positions.

The lack of an apparent consensus among empirical studies may lower the contribution of research to policy decisions. It encourages skepticism about the value of this research in guiding policy and raises questions about the basic economic concepts underlying demand analysis. In the absence of any clear statistical evidence about demand elasticities, policy makers are inclined to rely on intuition or noneconomic criteria. It is not our intention to remove all skepticism about elasticities; on the contrary, a certain amount of skepticism is useful if it leads to judicious use of this concept or to caution in selecting among available policy instruments. The primary purpose of this report is served if it helps the reader to understand the nature of the price effect and the value of information contained in current studies of demand, not only for major energy products, but for other products as well.

A second goal is to examine the importance of a number of empirical problems involved in estimating demand relationships, and to evaluate the effectiveness of econometric methods in dealing with them. These problems are not restricted to energy, but arise in econometric analyses of demand for any commodity. Energy demand provides a unique opportunity to explore them, however, because of the unusually large number of studies undertaken in recent years and the wide variety of econometric methods that have been employed. The literature on energy demand analysis therefore provides a case study of applied econometric analysis that can be useful in addressing the same issues in other applications.

The differences among statistical estimates of price elasticities arise from two basic sources: differences in the economic and institutional conditions reflected in the sample and differences in the procedure applied to the data to derive the estimates. Differences associated with the sample are generally easier to identify and understand. Estimates will vary across studies because the magnitudes and behavior of observed variables are different; the variables included in the model are different; consumer tastes and life styles in the observation period have changed; the stock of energy-using capital has changed; and institutional factors governing energy markets have changed. Just as these differences among samples may produce variations among estimates, so they will account for errors in forecasting behavior in future periods when the structure of demand has changed from the sample period.

Differences that arise because of estimation procedure are poorly understood and more difficult to identify, and thus are the primary focus of this study. Every econometric study of demand begins with the same basic economic concepts. It is the estimation procedure that produces divergence. A choice has to be made about the type of model to use, the kinds of data that are appropriate, and the estimation technique that fits the model and data. In making these choices, a number of estimation problems are either explicitly or implicitly addressed. These problems are discussed in detail in the next chapter.

This study investigates the relationship between estimation procedures used in studies of energy demand and the statistical results obtained. We wish to determine whether the choice of procedures accounts for the disparities among estimates of price elasticities of demand. To the extent that this accounts for differences, it removes a certain amount of skepticism about these studies.

There still remains the question of which procedures yield the more reliable estimates. To this end, it is necessary to ascertain the empirical importance of several methodological issues. What difference does it make whether a static or dynamic model is used? How important is aggregation bias? Is it useful to attempt to separate supply from demand effects? Are more sophisticated estimation techniques worth the trouble? The theoretical literature on econometric methods demonstrates the conditions under which estimators will be subject to aggregation bias, simultaneous equation bias, and assorted other sources of estimation error. Yet, one cannot deduce from the theoretical arguments the importance of the error or, in some cases, even the direction of the error. These are questions that require empirical verification.

The literature on energy demand is unusually rich in the number of studies that can be compared on the basis of estimation method, model specification, and sample data. It is rare to find such a wide variety of econometric studies investigating the same subject from different angles. What appears to be a confusing array of studies and statistical results can be used to advantage in exploring the sources of the confusion. Our intention is to use this information to shed light on the reasons for the disparities among empirical results and on the empirical importance of the estimation procedure.

A comparison of demand studies makes it possible to determine how sensitive the estimates are to their particular sets of conditions and methodology. The less sensitive a result is to specific economic conditions, the more confidently it can be used in forecasting exercises, as future conditions will undoubtedly differ from those existing during the sample period. Similarly, the less sensitive the result to estimation method, the less concern one may have for employing less convenient and more expensive approaches.

A final objective of this exercise is to provide an overall review and evaluation of the econometric literature on energy demand that can be used as a reference. This may assist practitioners in understanding the pitfalls as well as the successes of available estimates, and provide a basis for selecting among the results. The evaluation is intended to highlight the difficult conceptual problems, the progress in overcoming them, and the gaps that remain.

Chapter 2 presents the analytical basis for comparing and evaluating the econometric studies of energy demand. Starting from the economic concepts of demand common to these studies, the discussion focuses on the major methodological issues that arise in translating the theory into testable hypotheses about demand behavior: (1) the method of capturing the dynamics of demand; (2) the choice of the level of aggregation of the data; (3) the separation of supply and demand effects; (4) the choice of equation form and estimation technique; and (5) the identification of separate influences on demand.

The way in which these issues are addressed may be said to characterize a study's procedural approach. For example, one may choose to estimate the demand for a specific fuel directly with a reduced-form model, or indirectly with a model of structural components. The model may be static or dynamic, and may be applied to aggregate consumer behavior or to individual consumers. The model may ignore supply effects or attempt to integrate supply explicitly in an equilibrium relationship. The sample of data may be time-series, cross-section, or both. The choice of variables included may vary, the variables can be measured differently, and they may be combined in different functional forms. Chapter 2 describes these alternative estimation procedures, and the methodological questions they are intended to address.

Chapters 3 through 6 discuss studies pertaining to electricity, natural gas, petroleum, and coal, according to consuming sector (residential, commercial, industrial, transportation, and electricity generation) and by modeling technique and type of data analyzed. This organization is intended to group the statistical results by common procedure and data in order to highlight their similarities and differences.

The similarities and differences among statistical results are recorded largely in terms of the magnitude of estimated coefficients, their sign, their statistical significance, and their consistency with theory and intuition. These are associated with the estimation procedures and sample characteristics of the studies. Frequently, the associations cannot be sharply delineated. That is, each study embodies a large number of estimation features, some of which are common to other studies and some of which are not. It is not always clear which disparities among results can be identified with which features. Consequently, many conclusions drawn from this exercise follow from broad patterns that show up across a large variety of studies.

As for the range of studies included here, the first criterion is that the study incorporate a price effect on consumption behavior. In addition, consumption must be identified with one of the four energy product categories and with a specific consuming sector (including transportation). This excludes a number of important studies concerned with substitution in production between energy as an aggregate input and other factors of production, or substitution in consumption between energy and other commodity groups. Within the chosen range, an attempt was made to include all prominent studies currently available, but the choices are inherently subjective and some possibly important studies may have been overlooked. Finally, the studies included are not thoroughly or uniformly discussed, because the focus is on information bearing on the estimation issues rather than details about energy demand. Readers are referred to the original works for full details.

The last chapter draws a number of conclusions about the empirical results and estimation methods reviewed. The conclusions about measures of price elasticity focus on the question of reliability and which measures may be regarded as most defensible. The discussion of empirical methods concentrates on the relative efficacy of alternative estimation techniques and the implications of several estimation problems in measuring elasticities. The chapter closes with a discussion of some limitations of econometric analysis and their implications for users of these analyses.

chapter 2

Estimating the Demand for Energy:
Issues and Methodologies

The demand for energy is in principle no different than that for any other commodity, and the statistical analysis is based on the same economic concepts. Estimation of statistical demand relationships for energy products, moreover, will encounter the same range of methodological issues as that for any other commodity, although there are characteristics of energy demand, institutional features of energy markets, and problems of measurement of pertinent variables that require special attention in analyzing energy markets. The choice of analytical approaches and the way these special problems are addressed may influence the outcome of the analysis.

This chapter reviews the major methodological problems of estimation and the options available to deal with them. It begins with a brief discussion of the basic economic concept of demand and then turns to the problems of statistical inference. The major issues discussed here provide the basis for comparing and analyzing the empirical studies in the following chapters.

The Concept of Demand

All studies of demand elasticities are based on the same fundamental economic principles of demand in a competitive market.[1] At the

[1]Two venerable references which still warrant reading are Hicks (1939) and Samuelson (1965). Of more recent vintage is Malinvaud (1972).

7

simplest level, energy consumption by households is dependent on relative fuel prices and household income while that by firms is dependent on the level of output and relative input prices. These relationships are common to all econometric studies of energy demand and are derived from the principles of demand. Therefore the basic principles are discussed before turning to the complications.

Individual demand functions

It is usually assumed that consumers seek to allocate expenditures of income among available commodities so as to obtain the greatest degree of satisfaction from total expenditure, while producers demand energy inputs in relation to other factors of production in order to minimize the total costs of producing a given amount of goods. This difference in motivation means that an analysis of household energy consumption should be treated separately from an analysis of commercial and industrial use.

The basis for consumer demand is somewhat vague in that consumer satisfaction is determined by unknown individual preferences for different commodities that are generally regarded as given and constant during the period of analysis. It is assumed that an incremental increase in the consumption of a good, with the consumption of other goods constant, yields a positive increment in satisfaction, but that this increment or "marginal utility" declines as the quantity of consumption increases. For given preferences, the collection of goods which yields the maximum satisfaction must satisfy the condition that the marginal utility per dollar paid for each good be the same. If the marginal utility per dollar is greater for good A than for good B, then transferring a dollar of expenditure from B to A will increase total utility for the same total expenditure. It follows that a reduction in the relative price of good A will tend to increase the demand for good A, and vice versa; that is, the quantity consumed of a given commodity is inversely related to its price.

A producer's demand for energy inputs in production is similarly vague in that the constraints on production processes are usually unknown and regarded as given and constant during the period of analysis. These constraints include (1) technical limitations on production, which specify the maximum amount of outputs that can be produced with given amounts of inputs;[2] (2) limited availability of some inputs within a given time frame, where the "long run" is defined as a length of time in which all inputs are variable and the "short run" is the time period in which the maximum amount of some inputs, such as plant capacity, may be fixed; (3) constraints on the "divisibility" of inputs and outputs, because technology is not "continuous," so that small variations in inputs cannot be smoothly transformed into small variations in outputs, or because it may be impossible to buy certain inputs or sell certain outputs other than in discrete "lumps."[3] The optimal input and output bundles for the producer, subject to these constraints, must satisfy two conditions similar to those for the consumer. First, production of any good will be expanded until an additional increment of the good produced in the most efficient manner makes no further contribution to net revenue. Second, employment of any factor of production will be increased until, other inputs remaining unchanged, an additional unit of the factor yields no additional net revenue.

For a firm with only one output, these conditions can be put in simpler form. The available technology specifies which combinations of inputs can produce any level of output. For a given level of output the producer will choose that input combination where the increment to output per dollar is the same for all inputs; otherwise, by shifting out of one input and into another the same output can be produced at lower cost. This yields a cost function, relating to each output the minimum total payment to factors required to produce that output. Then to maximize net revenue, the firm will choose that output such

[2]When the number of outputs exceeds one, the technical constraints specify a "frontier," a set of alternative output bundles producible with the given collection of inputs such that it is impossible to increase the output of any one good without reducing the output of one or more of the others. For example, two units of labor and one unit of machinery might be used to produce three tanks and two units of food or one tank and three units of food, but could not yield both three units of food and three tanks.

[3]Constraint (3) applies also to consumers in their purchases and sales of durable goods. Both (2) and (3) can be regarded as examples of market failure in the sense that well-organized markets for used durable goods, like capital in place, or the services of single-family dwellings versus the dwellings themselves, means consumers could be regarded as entrepreneurs who buy durable goods and rent to themselves the services of these goods. This, however, does not solve the empirical problem of determining the margin to which these activities are taken; if organized markets are absent the rental rates individual charge themselves for the services cannot be directly observed.

that marginal cost, the additional cost incurred by an increment to production, equals marginal revenue, the incremental change in gross receipts from changing production. If marginal revenue exceeds marginal cost, net revenue will increase with larger output. Having specified an optimal output, the firm chooses among input bundles technically capable of producing this output so that the "marginal conditions" among inputs described above are satisfied. Thus, a reduction in the relative price of an input, given the level of output, will lead to an increase in the use of that input; an increase in the level of output, given input prices, may lead to an increase in the use of all inputs.

The above characterizations of optimal behavior are relevant under very general market conditions. Indeed, it is not even assumed that organized markets exist for the various goods; it is only necessary that consumers know their tastes, producers know their technology, and all agents know how much of the goods they can buy or sell at various prices. (These amounts could vary among agents for the same prices.) Under the special conditions of "perfect competition," individual producer decisions will be completely determined by technical production conditions and prices, while individual consumer decisions will be completely determined by tastes, prices, and incomes. These conditions are that (1) all potential traders face the same price for each good; (2) no single trader's decision can affect this price, and (3) individual traders can buy or sell as much of each good as they wish (and can afford) at the given prices.

If these conditions prevail, then demand functions that depend on prices and incomes for consumers and prices and output for producers can be derived from the "marginal conditions." For example, the cost of the "marginal unit" of a good to a consumer is usually the market price, so for any set of prices a consumer will demand a bundle of goods such that the ratio of marginal utility to price is the same for each good.[4] Each set of factor prices determines (with given technology) the least-cost combination of inputs capable of producing a given amount of output; that is, factor prices specify the cost function. Since marginal revenue equals the market price for the competitive producer, the

---

[4]Consumers of electricity and natural gas face a price schedule rather than a single price, which complicates the estimation and interpretation of demand elasticities. This will be discussed further below.

condition "marginal cost equals marginal revenue" determines the quantity produced as a function of output, price, and indirectly through the cost function, input prices. Input demand functions are determined from the "marginal conditions" and depend on both input prices and the choice of the output level.

With a change in one of these fundamental parameters (income, product prices, or input prices), consumers and producers will move to a new equilibrium position. In a static demand analysis, the new and the old positions are compared to determine the magnitude of the change. Decision makers are assumed to make immediate adjustments, unhindered by market supply lags or lack of perfect information. In dynamic demand analysis, the focus of concern is the path of movement from one equilibrium to another. This process may require changes in capital stock (e.g., housing stock or automobile fleet) over a long period of time. Other factors and market conditions will affect the adjustment process and determine if and how a new static equilibrium may be achieved.

Market demand functions

On the basis of the discussion so far, one can estimate consumer demand functions for a given energy product using information about the individual's income and relative commodity prices. However, there is little interest in the characteristics of demand for a single individual, as that individual may behave quite differently from other consumers, nor are systematic records kept of individual consumption behavior over time. Of greater interest is consumption behavior of groups of individuals or groups of firms. Proceeding from the demand function for an individual consumer to the demand function for a group of consumers requires some form of aggregation over individual consuming units. What is important for statistical demand analysis is that any aggregation requires assumptions about the similarity of individual consumers which, if incorrect, introduce the possibility of errors in the results.

Demand functions for groups of consumers are referred to as market demand functions. Market demand functions may be derived from a summation of individual demands under special conditions. If the market is competitive, if all buyers face the same market price, and if all other variables but price and quantity demanded are constant, the aggregate relation can be obtained by summing at each price the values of all individual purchases. Prices and quantities for the entire market are related in the same fashion as prices and quantities for individuals. If any one of the premises does not hold, market demand is not a simple sum of individuals' demands. For example, if individual consumers react to changes in income differently in their purchases of energy products, aggregate consumer demand for energy products will not have the same form as individual demand relations. Similarly, if different firms relate energy inputs to outputs in different proportions, aggregate industry demand is not a simple sum of individual firms' demands when output changes.

Even where aggregate market demand is a simple linear sum of individuals' demands, it does not follow that market demand elasticities will necessarily equal the "typical" or average elasticities of individual consumers and firms. Market demand elasticities will differ from individual consumers' elasticities because different consumers enter or leave the market at different prices. Market consumption expands (or falls) as price falls (or rises) not only because some persons consume more (or less) but also because some consumers enter (or leave) the market. The distribution of entry points affects the shape and elasticity of the market function, so that market elasticities cannot be inferred directly from individual behavior.

The concept of market demand is further complicated if the process of aggregation involves different commodities as well as different consumers. Strictly speaking, the concept of demand applies to a single homogeneous commodity. If the analysis is applied to an aggregation of differentiable products, such as motor fuels obtained by summing over different types and grades of gasoline and diesel fuels, the demand for the aggregate involves the summing of individual demands that are not necessarily similar. Even more complicated are aggregate industrial demand relations in which both outputs and inputs are composites of heterogeneous products.

This concludes the brief review of the principles of demand. The next section defines some common terminology found throughout the rest of this book.

Definitions of elasticities

Demand elasticities refer to measures of the responsiveness of quantity demanded to changes in the determinants of demand. The own-price elasticity is the percentage change in quantity demanded resulting from a given percentage change in the price of the good in question, assuming all other factors affecting demand remain constant.[5] Elasticities with respect to other prices (termed cross-elasticities) and with respect to income and output (termed income and output elasticities) are similarly defined. Functions are called inelastic if price elasticities are less than one in absolute value; unit elastic if the elasticity is one; and elastic if the elasticity exceeds one. This terminology is reflected in categorizing goods purchased by consumers according to whether total spending on a good is positively or negatively related to its price. If demand is inelastic, total expenditures will be positively related to price changes; if demand is elastic, total expenditures will be negatively related to price changes; and if demand is unitary elastic, spending will be invariant with respect to the price changes.

Cross-elasticities are particularly important with respect to energy products, among different fuels because more than one fuel can be used for the same purpose, and between fuels and other factors of production because of their complementarity or substitutability in production processes. Because energy consumption is utilized in association with some durable good, the choice of the durable good as well as the type of fuel will depend on relative energy prices, durable goods prices, and prices of related commodities in consumption or production. Thus, for example, consumer demand for gasoline has a cross-elasticity relationship with the price of automobiles, the price of tires, the price of diesel fuel, the price of public transportation, and so on. Industrial demand for electricity may have a cross-relationship with the prices of fuel oil, coal, and natural gas, the prices of associated fuel-using equipment, the price of labor, and so on.

The cross-elasticity of fuel i with respect to fuel (or input) j is defined as the percentage change in the quantity demanded of i which results from a given percentage change in the price of fuel j. If the change in quantity of i is positively related to the price of j, the two fuels are called substitutes and if negatively related, the goods are called complements. This terminology applies only when two goods are

---

[5]Complications in the measurement of elasticities arise in practice because the percentage change occurs for discrete intervals rather than for infinitesimally small increments. Percentage changes will vary with the base values, such as the beginning or ending points of the interval or an average of the two. The latter is often recommended as a linear approximation of the average elasticity over an interval.

involved and the prices of all other goods are constant. When the number of goods involved exceeds two, the signs of pairwise cross-elasticities may not be mutually consistent with the above definition of complementarity and substitutability.[6] An alternative definition suggested by Allen (1938), called the partial elasticity of substitution, measures a compensated price change that holds income (in the case of consumers) or output (in the case of producers) constant as price changes. This measure is intended to eliminate the income effect of a price change that is included in the cross-price elasticity, but which may offset the substitution effect associated with the price change and give a sign that incorrectly defines the relationship between two goods. That is, instead of relying on the sign of $\partial Q_i / \partial P_j$, where Q_i is the quantity of fuel i and P_j is the price of fuel j, we observe the sign of

$$S_{ij} = \frac{\partial Q_i}{\partial P_j} + Q_j \frac{\partial Q_i}{\partial Y} \tag{2-1}$$

where Y is income (or output). If S_{ij} is positive, i and j are called substitutes; if negative, they are called complements. This definition sometimes creates confusion because the sign of S_{ij} may differ from the more intuitive definition given by the sign of the cross-price elasticity.

Dynamics of Demand for Energy Products

The fact that energy products are not consumed for their own sake, but in conjunction with energy-using equipment for the services provided, gives rise to two major issues in modeling demand. First, the demand for a specific fuel is interrelated with the demand for end-use services and the demand for associated fuel-using equipment. The demand for services depends on their costs; the demand for fuel-specific equipment depends on equipment prices and on relative operating costs; and the demands for each fuel depend on the total demand for services and the choice of fuel-using equipment. Prices both determine and are determined by the decisions made at each stage. There is, in other words, an interrelationship among various fuel prices,

[6]Cf. Samuelson (1974).

characteristics of stocks of fuel-using equipment, and the amounts of each fuel consumed. Where one focuses attention in this causal chain often determines the modeling approach taken (and also helps explain the variety of empirical models).

The second major issue is that the demand for fuels is time-oriented. Consumers are limited in their ability to respond immediately to a price change. Individuals, for example, reside in houses with a given array of appliances of given efficiency, own a given number and type of automobiles, and possess a given set of consumption habits. Their immediate response to a price change is limited to more or less use of available energy-using devices. Over a longer period of time, individuals may alter their stock of energy-using equipment, but only when the fuel price has increased enough to make the changes worthwhile. New residences and new equipment purchases will reflect the changes in energy prices more readily, and will combine with replacement purchases to gradually alter the stock of capital.

The same considerations apply to energy consumption behavior of firms. Firms are locked into existing capital structures and production processes, limiting their response to energy price changes to more or less intensive use of existing capital. As new plants are planned, or existing equipment is replaced, firms have a wider range of options with which to respond to the price change. Thus, the initial, or short-run, response to a price change is only a partial response, and the total response may be expected to cumulate over time. It also follows that measures of price elasticities of demand, to be meaningful, must be defined with respect to a period of time.

The interrelationships between fuel demands and capital stocks and the time dimension of consumption behavior are not separable issues. They are two aspects of the dynamic process of energy demand, although in the literature on demand they are often treated separately, with models designed to capture one or both aspects of the response to price changes. Two basic approaches are used: reduced-form fuel consumption models and structural models that derive fuel demands indirectly from the demand for fuel-using equipment.

Reduced-form fuel consumption models

The most common approach is to estimate fuel consumption directly in a reduced-form model that combines the elements of interfuel substitution and capital stock adjustments along with elements that affect the rate of utilization of existing stocks. These models implicitly or explicitly assume some adaptation of the following relationships. The consumption of fuel i may be expressed as

$$Q_i = f(A_i, R_i) \tag{2-2}$$

where A_i is the demand for equipment using fuel i (as derived from the demand for end-use services), and R_i is the rate of utilization of existing equipment stocks. Behavioral relations for these variables may be expressed as

$$A_i = g(P_i, P_j, P_a, Y, X) \tag{2-3}$$

$$R_i = L(P_i, Y, Z) \tag{2-4}$$

where P_i is the price of fuel i, P_j is the price of competing fuel j, P_a is the price of equipment, Y is income (if a final consumer) or output (if an intermediate consumer), and X and Z are other relevant variables. Substituting (2-3) and (2-4) in (2-2) gives the reduced-form equation

$$Q_i = k(P_i, P_j, P_a, Y, X, Z) \tag{2-5}$$

for fuel i, where optimization of equipment stocks is implicitly assumed.

The dependent variable in (2-5) may be normalized with respect to several alternative bases, depending on the consuming sector and the level of aggregation of the data. Residential consumption is usually normalized with respect to the number of households, persons, or customers in the observation unit. Commercial and industrial consumption is usually measured in terms of the total consumption for the observation unit, as average consumption makes less sense for these widely diverse sectors. Alternatively, consumption of each fuel may be normalized with respect to total energy consumption by the sector or end use.

The latter approach characterizes market share or fuel share models. They are intended to emphasize interfuel substitution for a given level of total energy demand or end-use consumption. The models of end-use categories differ little from the general form in equation (2-5) except for the definition of the dependent variable. In general, it is defined as the share of fuel i used for a given purpose. Data limitations restrict their use to the residential sector, in which the most common application concerns fuel shares for space heating.

The procedure for estimating market shares for each fuel and consuming sector involves two steps. First, total energy consumption by sector is estimated separately. These estimates are then used as the normalization base in the second stage, which estimates the share of total energy contributed by each fuel consumed by the sector. Several variations of the specific form of the relationship may be found, including a log-linear specification as in DOE (1978), a conditional logit specification as in Baughman and Joskow (1975) and Baughman and Zerhoot (1975), and a linear specification as in Chern (1976). The two-step decision process involving, first, total energy demand and, second, specific fuel demands, may be less appropriate than the reverse order, particularly in the long run when adjustments in fuel-using characteristics of the capital stocks occur.

All reduced-form models of the type given by equation (2-5) involve two major defects. First, adequate data are often not available about equipment prices and other characteristics of the capital stock. Second, when information is available, the model does not specify a behavioral process by which equilibrium adjustments in the stock of capital take place. There is no clear distinction between adjustments in utilization rates and adjustments in capital stocks. Thus, the model must be applied in such a way as to make the distinction.

The simplest method available for distinguishing between short-run partial adjustments and long-run equilibrium adjustments involves the type of sample data employed. Time-series data are used to reflect the incomplete adjustments over time to a sequence of changes in prices. This approach assumes that the structure of the model applies without change over the entire sample period. Cross-section data are used to reflect long-run equilibrium adjustments to persistent price differentials across groups of consuming units. This approach assumes that the data reflect equilibrium adjustments to price differences and that the structure of the model remains valid across diverse consuming groups. The more diverse the cross-sectional groups, the more questionable the assumption of similar behavioral relationships. Cross-country samples, for example, are typically less similar in this respect than cross-regions in the same country. In addition, cross-sectional data are not likely to reflect steady-state patterns, but rather states of differential disequilibria, because the demand process involves capital stock adjustments that occur continuously over long periods of time within each cross-sectional grouping.

Another approach designed to distinguish between short-run and long-run consumption behavior, and yet avoid the requirement for data on capital stocks, is the so-called lag adjustment model. The model is motivated in several different ways, but they all reduce to an estimating equation that includes lagged values of the dependent variable as an explanatory variable. One version is the well-known Koyck (1954) model, which specifies consumption as a function of lagged prices, as in

$$Q_t = a_0 + a_1 \sum_{i=0}^{\infty} \lambda^i P_{t-i} + u_t, \qquad 0 < \lambda < 1 \qquad (2\text{-}6)$$

where the weights attached to each lagged price sum to unity and decline geometrically as they move back in time, and u_t is a random error term. It is well known that this specification reduces to[7]

$$Q_t = a_0 (1 - \lambda) + a_1 (1 - \lambda) P_t + \lambda Q_{t-1} + (u_t - \lambda u_{t-1}) \quad (2\text{-}7)$$

If the variables are measured in logarithms, the short-run price elasticity of demand is given by $a_1 (1 - \lambda)$ and the long-run elasticity is given by $a_1 = [a_1 (1 - \lambda)/(1 - \lambda)]$. Furthermore, the mean of the series λ^i is given by $\lambda/(1 - \lambda)$, which may be taken as a measure of the average adjustment period.

The same estimating equation follows if consumption is hypothesized to depend on expected prices rather than actual prices, and expected prices are determined on the basis of a distributed lag of past prices, as in

$$P_t^e = \sum_{i=0}^{\infty} \lambda^i P_{t-i} \qquad (2\text{-}8)$$

Again, λ takes on a value between zero and unity, so the weights decline geometrically with time, indicating that recent prices are most important in the formation of expectations than past prices.

[7]See Johnston (1972), chapter 10.

Another variation of the lagged adjustment model is the partial adjustment version introduced by Houthakker and Taylor (1970), where desired consumption (Q_t^*) is specified as a log-linear function of price and other variables (Z_t) and disturbance (ϵ_t), as

$$Q_t^* = b_0 + b_1P_t + b_2Z_t + \epsilon_t \qquad (2\text{-}9)$$

To put the model in operational form containing only observable variables, an adjustment process relating actual and desired consumption is assumed:

$$Q_t = Q_{t-1} + \gamma \, (Q_t^* - Q_{t-1}) \text{ for } 0 < \gamma \leq 1 \qquad (2\text{-}10)$$

That is, in the current period the consumer will move only part of the way from the initial position Q_{t-1} to the desired position Q_t^* in response to a price change. The closer γ is to unity, the faster the adjustment process. Combining (2-9) and (2-10) gives

$$Q_t = b_0\gamma + b_1\gamma P_t + (1 + \gamma)Q_{t-1} + b_2\gamma Z_t + \epsilon_t \qquad (2\text{-}11)$$

which is of the same form as the Koyck model, but with a simpler disturbance term.

The lag specifications are simple and convenient because they provide an estimate of the lagged effect of price changes with just two coefficients, and require no information on changes in the capital stocks. The procedure is *ad hoc,* however, with no underlying theory of adjustment to justify the declining geometric pattern. The largest response to any price change need not occur in the first period, nor decline geometrically thereafter. Moreover, when the model is expanded to include additional explanatory variables—such as competing fuel prices, income, and noneconomic variables—the same lag coefficient is used to obtain all long-run parameters. The lag response of household consumption, for example, is assumed to be the same for prices, income, climatic, and demographic variables.

The Koyck procedure has the disadvantage of introducing serial correlation in the residuals even if they are independently distributed in their original form. A nonzero covariance is also created between the lagged value of the dependent variable used as an explanatory variable and the residual term. The second problem creates a small sample bias in least-squares estimates, while the first problem implies that the bias will not disappear in large samples. Moreover, the conventional Durbin–Watson statistic used to test for serial correlation loses power, giving values biased toward that of a random disturbance. Consistent estimation procedures are available, but their small sample results may be subject to unacceptable error. The flow adjustment version yields a simpler error term that raises fewer estimation difficulties, unless ϵ_t is serially correlated to begin with. This is likely to be the case in pooled samples of time-series and cross-section data, as cross-sectional differences tend to persist over time. In any case, the presence of Q_{t-1} still creates a bias problem for small samples.

The partial adjustment formulation focuses on another aspect of the lag adjustment approach that encounters frequent criticism. The model assumes that consumers react to a price change by continuously adjusting actual purchases of durable goods to some desired stock over time. However, the nature of the acquisition process is often one of discrete consumer choices, where the consumer either has or does not have a given appliance. Aggregation over discrete consumer decisions may produce a smoothing effect on a market level response function, but no attempt has been made to rationalize a market function of the geometric form specified by the lag adjustment models.

Finally, it will become evident in the review of empirical results that the lag adjustment models are highly sensitive to variations in model specification. Even minor changes in equation form, variable definition, and sample period tend to produce major changes in estimates of the coefficient of the lagged dependent variable. Consequently, estimates of long-run elasticities tend to be highly erratic.

A distributed-lag model that avoids the lagged dependent variable is based upon the Almon (1965) polynomial lag scheme, as given by

$$Q_t = a + \sum_{i=0}^{k} b_i \, P_{t-i} + \sum_{i=0}^{m} c_i \, Z_{t-i} \qquad\qquad (2\text{-}12)$$

where consumption is determined by prices over the past k periods and by the vector of other independent variables over the past m periods, where the length of the lags (k and m) must be specified. The procedure is based on the Weierstrass theorem that a continuous function can be approximated by a polynomial of degree less than the function in a closed interval. The theorem provides no indication of the degree of the polynomial required for a specified level of accuracy, but a number of different values may be tried for a judgment as to which fits best. The short-run (one-period) demand response to price is given by the coefficients of the first lag term, b_0, and the long-run price response by the sum of all coefficients, $b_0 + b_1 + b_2 + \ldots + b_k$. Price elasticities can then be calculated by multiplying the price response by P/Q.

This procedure avoids the problems associated with a lagged dependent variable, but it is nevertheless an *ad hoc* procedure in that the shape of the polynomial is determined by the data. It is a matter of choosing the result that best fits the data, rather than using the data to test a hypothesis about the nature of the adjustment process. This is a general criticism of distributed-lag models and is important in that test statistics may not be interpreted with the usual probabilistic meaning.

A common criticism of the reduced-form consumption models is that they are merely intuitive representations of the basic principles of demand but are not based upon a specific hypothesis about consumer preferences or producer costs. A relatively new procedure seeks to overcome this gap between theory and estimation by using the dual relationship between prices and quantities in the theory of demand.[8] The application of this procedure to a firm's demand for energy inputs provides an illustration of the simplifying assumptions often required for estimation.[9]

It is assumed that a twice-differentiable production function exists for each industry j,

$$O_j = F_j (E, X) \tag{2-13}$$

where O_j is total output, E is a vector of energy inputs, and X is a vector of nonenergy inputs. The lack of information on the elements of X often forces the researcher to develop energy demand functions that are independent of nonenergy inputs. This is achieved by assuming the production function is weakly separable in energy inputs, so that (2-13) may be written as

$$O_j = F_j [H_j(E), X] \tag{2-14}$$

[8]See Christensen, Jorgenson, and Lau (1973, 1975).
[9]See, for example, Halvorsen (1978), chapter 6.

where H_j is an aggregate energy input function for the jth industry. The energy cost function dual to the energy input fraction may be written as

$$W_j = W_j (H_j, P_e) \tag{2-15}$$

where P_e is a vector of prices of fuels included in E, and H_j is an index of aggregate energy input in the industry.

The next problem is estimating H_j because of problems of aggregating over individual fuels to obtain a valid measure of aggregate energy input, particularly in the context of a model where changes in fuel composition are part of the problem. The problem can be avoided by estimating unit cost functions for energy inputs rather than total cost functions. The procedure requires that the energy input function in (2-15) be a positive nondecreasing, linear homogeneous, concave function such that it may be written as

$$W_j = H_j \cdot V_j(P_e) \tag{2-16}$$

where V_j may be interpreted as the unit cost function for energy inputs in the jth industry.

Diewert (1974) has shown that the demand for the ith energy input may be obtained from a partial derivative of V_j with respect to the price of the ith input, as in

$$\frac{\partial V_j}{\partial P_i} = \frac{X_i}{H_j} \tag{2-17}$$

where X_i may be interpreted as the cost-minimizing quantity of input i. Own-price elasticities of demand for fuel i are given by

$$E_{ii} = \frac{\partial X_i}{\partial P_i} \frac{P_i}{X_i} \tag{2-18}$$

and the cross-price elasticities of demand for fuel i with respect to fuel k are given by

$$E_{ik} = \frac{\partial X_i}{\partial P_k} \frac{P_k}{X_i} \tag{2-19}$$

Because these elasticities are based on a unit cost function, they assume total energy input is held constant. They measure, therefore, only a partial response to a price change, as total energy consumption may change as well. Total elasticities may be calculated as

$$E_{ii}^{t} = E_{ii} + E_{ih} E_{hi} \tag{2-20}$$

$$E_{ik}^{t} = E_{ik} + E_{ih} E_{hk} \tag{2-21}$$

where E_{ii} and E_{ik} are given in equations (2-18) and (2-19), E_{ih} is the elasticity of demand for fuel i as total energy consumption changes, and E_{hi} is the elasticity of demand for total energy consumption with respect to the price of fuel i. Thus, a great deal more information is required than that obtained by estimating input demand functions in (2-17).

If the aggregate energy input function (2-16) is linear homogeneous, Halvorsen (1978) demonstrates that E_{ih} equals unity and the estimation problem is reduced. In addition, as noted by Halvorsen, E_{hi} may be expressed in terms of the elasticity of demand for aggregate energy with respect to the price of aggregate energy, times the cost share of fuel i. However, as we shall discuss further below, aggregates of different fuels and their prices are not particularly meaningful, and estimates of total energy elasticities must be viewed with suspicion.

A final issue that is deferred until later is the assumed form of V_j from which the estimating equations are derived. The estimates are dependent on the specific form utilized, and all available choices involve a certain amount of arbitrariness.

Structural demand models

The structural demand models attempt to estimate the separate components that combine to derive the reduced-form models, such as the behavioral relations represented by equations (2-3) and (2-4). A variety of different approaches are used. The most common is to estimate changes in utilization rates directly from a short-run consumption model like one of those described in the preceding section. Long-run adjustments to changes in fuel prices are then derived separately from a durable goods demand model. As yet, these models have been applied only to residential fuel demands (including gasoline) because of the lack of data for the commercial and industrial sectors, so our examples refer to household appliances and automobiles.

Fisher and Kaysen (1962) developed one of the earliest structural modeling efforts. The demand for a given fuel (in this case, electricity) in time period t is given by

$$Q_t = \sum_{i=1}^{n} K_{it} W_{it} \tag{2-22}$$

where W_{it} is the average stock of the ith appliance that uses the fuel in question and K_{it} is the average intensity of use of the ith appliance. In the short run W_{it} is taken as fixed, so analysis of changes in Q_t is focused on K_{it}. The determinants of K_{it} include relative prices and income, following the basic principles of demand discussed earlier.

In the long run, W_{it} will change in response to relative fuel prices. Fisher and Kaysen reject the flow adjustment type of model applied to changes in W_{it} because the stock held by an individual cannot vary continuously over time. Rather, individuals purchasing the ith appliance typically hold a zero stock. They consider instead the ratio W_{it}/W_{it-1} as a measure of the growth of stocks to be explained. The ratio will be independent of the size of the stock alone, assuming the number of people owning the ith appliance this year is proportional to the number owning it last year. Relative ownership will vary according to, among other things, some ratio of an index of living standards; the ratio of households capable of using the appliance (as indicated, for example, by the number of wired households or gas hookups); the ratio of incomes; appliance prices; and fuel prices. Separate and independent equations were estimated for each of five household appliances.

A major problem with the Fisher–Kaysen model is an appropriate measure of appliance stocks. Even with accurate sales figures for each period, it is difficult to construct an index that appropriately reflects changes in the age or quality of appliance stocks. Furthermore, Fisher and Kaysen estimate their model with a time series of cross-state observations, and characteristics of appliance stocks vary widely by state. The poor quality of appliance data is in part to blame for the generally poor statistical results, where price variables failed to show any observable influence over changes in appliance stocks. Halvorsen (1975) argues that the poor results are due to the specification Fisher and Kaysen use.

Another variation of the basic model has been developed by Taylor, Blattenberger, and Verleger (1977). The short-run utilization rate model is the basic lagged adjustment fuel consumption model, but with consumption divided by a measure of appliance stocks as the dependent variable. The index of appliance stocks is a weighted sum of all major appliances using the fuel in question (in this case, electricity), with the weight for the ith appliance given by

$$W_i = \frac{U_i}{\Sigma U_i} \tag{2-23}$$

and U_i represents the normal utilization rate for the ith appliance, measured by fuel consumption per unit of time.

The capital stock equations, one for each of ten appliances, attempt to explain variations in the stock of appliances in each period as a function of the log of various economic and noneconomic variables, plus the lagged measure of the stock of appliances. Thus, contrary to the reasoning given above, Taylor et al. attempt to estimate a flow adjustment version of the basic Fisher–Kaysen model. Again, the results are poor and indicate little price sensitivity.

Anderson (1974) attempts to avoid the problem of measuring existing appliance stocks by focusing attention on the share of new appliances that use a specific fuel. The share of new purchases of appliance j using fuel i is posited as a function of relative fuel and appliance prices, income, and a number of other variables reflecting demographic and residence characteristics. The estimating equations, called appliance saturation equations, are normalized by taking the ratio of two fuel shares. The choice of fuel in the denominator does not matter in principle, but statistical results vary with the combination. The appliance equations reveal important price effects, but not consistently for all appliances. Taking a weighted average of the significant price coefficients for each appliance, Anderson derives estimates of appliance saturation demand elasticities. Fuel consumption elasticities are then obtained by adding the saturation elasticities to utilization rate price elasticities, where the latter are obtained from a standard reduced-form model of residential consumption for each fuel.

McFadden, Puig, and Kirshner (1977) have developed the most successful, if not the most sophisticated, analysis of residential demand, using a conditional logit model to reflect discrete consumer choice decisions. The model's success may be the result of a superior data base, as they make use of a 1975 survey of households concerning fuel consumption, appliance stocks, and several other economic and noneconomic characteristics.

Their two-equation approach follows the same logic as above. Short-run price elasticities are derived from an appliance utilization model, which is a static reduced-form consumption model (though with other interesting adaptations that will be discussed further below). Long-run price elasticities are obtained from the sum of the utilization rate elasticities and the appliance saturation demand elasticities. The appliance saturation equations estimate the share of households owning a given appliance portfolio, where the determinants of ownership include price, income, and other variables. The household survey provides a rich source of information on appliance saturation rates to apply to their model, and the results are most successful in confirming the influence of various characteristics of equipment stocks on energy consumption behavior.

The two-equation model of utilization rates and durable goods demand is also found among studies of gasoline demand. Burright and Enns (1975) use the procedure to estimate, first, a short-run equation for gasoline consumption and, second, changes in the demand for autos that are associated with gasoline prices. The auto demand model fails to distinguish between classes of fuel-efficient options, and thus cannot reveal the important changes in the composition of the auto fleet that may result from fuel price increases.

An alternative approach developed by Cato, Rodekohr, and Sweeney (1976) estimates vehicle-miles traveled in place of the standard reduced-form model of gasoline consumption to determine the price effect on utilization rates. Because gasoline consumption is equal to vehicle-miles traveled divided by average miles per gallon of the stock of autos, and the stock of autos is fixed in the short run, the short-run price elasticity of consumption is derived from the elasticity of vehicle-miles traveled.

In the long run, rising gasoline prices lead to an improvement in the fuel efficiency of the fleet of autos. To estimate this effect, the authors first estimate the demand for new cars by three size classes. The new car demands for each class are then weighted by average miles per gallon for each class and summed together to give the new car fleet weighted average miles per gallon. Next, the weighted average miles per gallon of the entire stock of autos is obtained by adding the new car average to the existing stock, which is in turn vintaged with exponential scrappage rates. The long-run effect of price on average mileage, plus the short-run effect on vehicle-miles traveled, give the combined long-run price effect on gasoline consumption.

Comparing model specifications

The structural models just described are theoretically more pleasing and potentially more informative than the reduced-form models because they separate the dynamic elements of demand and permit the identification of the sources of consumption behavior. But whether they work better in practice depends on the quality of the data and the robustness of the estimators, among other things. This is a matter that can be evaluated only by a comparison of empirical results. The nature of the modeling technique is therefore one important criterion by which to compare and evaluate various estimates of demand elasticities. Of central importance in this comparison is whether the magnitudes of elasticity estimates correspond in any way to the analytical technique employed.

There is also a matter of practical convenience involved in the comparison, as the reduced-form models are considerably less cumbersome to use and, particularly at the more aggregative levels, require a great deal less data. If the structural models and reduced-form models yield similar results, or are equally inconclusive, the reduced-form models have the advantage of simplicity. Finally, there is a purely methodological reason for comparing the empirical results of different models. Because of the topical importance of energy demand behavior, there is a great deal more overlapping and redundant research available in this area than for virtually any other product category. The energy demand literature therefore presents a unique opportunity to compare the performance of different analytical approaches applied to the same problem.

Aggregation and Measurement Problems

The theory of demand is defined in terms of individual units consuming homogeneous commodities, but our interest, and usually the data, relate to groups of consumers purchasing a category of heterogeneous products for a variety of uses. Estimating the demand for a specific fuel inevitably requires some form of aggregation. Even with the finest detail micro data, one must aggregate over different end uses to obtain a measure of the price responsiveness of each fuel. Often the only available consumption data combine the activities of different consumers, where each may have different uses for the same fuel as well as different propensities for consumption in each application. Residential demand for electricity, for example, is comprised of the demands for electricity by different individuals for such diverse purposes as space heating, water heating, air conditioning, lighting, and for powering a variety of other household appliances. Individual households do not all have the same array of electrical appliances, nor the same propensity for utilizing them.

The characteristics of individual consumers in the industrial and commercial sectors are even more diverse than in the residential sector. Firms use fuels in different ways to produce different end products. The commercial sector includes retail establishments, office buildings, apartment buildings, government buildings, and light industry among the many types of consumers. Aggregate industrial consumption is perhaps the extreme case because of the substantial difference in the way energy may be used for production by different industrial firms. Some are large energy-intensive operations and others may be small and less intensive. Even firms within the same industrial group may use different fuels, in different intensities, depending on the range of technical options. Each application possesses different demand characteristics, with some that are fuel-specific and requiring substantial modifications of the capital stock, and others with considerable flexibility in fuel switching.

Because the demand for a given fuel will involve some degree of aggregation, the implications for extending the theory beyond the micro level should be addressed. It is well known that a simple linear summation over individuals and commodities produces two basic difficulties.[10] First, the parameters of the aggregate relation in general

[10]See, for example, Allen (1960), chapter 20.

will depend, not only on the corresponding parameters of the micro relations, but also on a combination of noncorresponding parameters. The price elasticity parameters of micro relations, in other words, need not carry over as aggregate price elasticity parameters in the aggregate relation. Second, regression estimates of coefficients of the aggregate relation are subject to an aggregation bias. Specifically, the expected value of the aggregate parameter estimate is equal to the sum of the individual parameters plus one or more covariance terms involving the micro parameters. The empirical question is: under what conditions may the aggregation error be eliminated, or at least become tolerable? The formal requirements for groupings are very restrictive, though there are approximation procedures requiring weaker assumptions that may be sufficiently accurate in certain contexts. A variety of alternative conditions have been presented.

Avoiding errors in aggregating over commodities, according to the composite commodity theorem developed by Hicks (1939) and Leontief (1936), requires that relative prices of individual commodities in the group remain constant. Alternatively, Gorman (1953, 1959) and Strotz (1959) have demonstrated that composite commodity groupings require, among other conditions, that individual utility functions (or production functions) be strongly separable. Strongly separable means that changes in prices and incomes (or output) will not affect the proportion of expenditures on each good within each group. If two goods belong to different groups, for example, the marginal utility associated with each is independent of the quantities consumed of the other good. So restrictive is the strong separability condition that, as Brown and Deaton (1972, p. 1166) point out, "it is even possible to calculate price elasticities without observing any variation in prices."

More recently, Barten (1970) showed that satisfactory aggregate demand functions can be constructed on the basis of the assumption of weak separability. In this case, for any two goods belonging to a commodity group, the ratio of their marginal utilities is assumed to be independent of the quantity consumed of any good outside the group. Barten's aggregation procedure involves the use of price and quantity indices using group value shares and marginal budget shares as weights. In practice, little is known about marginal budget shares so average budget shares are used instead. But average and marginal budget shares are equal only if utility is strongly separable.

Aggregation over individual demand functions is also troublesome. Gorman (1953) has shown that it is necessary that all consumers within the same group have identical income elasticities in order to construct an aggregate demand function. When this condition holds, the aggregate demand function will depend on the individual demand functions plus the distribution of consumers over price and income. Pearce (1964) has demonstrated that weaker conditions will satisfy the treatment of groups as the single consumer of demand theory. However, as Brown and Deaton (1972, p. 1170) conclude, "the balance of probability is against individuals or groups of individuals acting 'ideally' so as to give rise to aggregate equations which satisfy, even approximately, the conditions for correct aggregations."

This is not a very encouraging situation. The best guide is simply to work with the least aggregative samples of the most homogeneous groups possible. Beyond this, there is not much one can do but be alert to the possibilities of estimation errors. The degree to which different levels of aggregation, or different kinds of aggregation, will affect estimation results is an empirical question that can be assessed only with empirical evidence. Theory tells us only that an error may be introduced, but cannot tell us how important it is, and often cannot tell us the direction of the bias. For this reason, many empirical studies simply ignore the possibility of aggregation errors and concentrate instead on sampling and specification errors, which are more amenable to standard econometric methods. For the same reason it is important to distinguish among the empirical studies by the level and kind of aggregation employed. By doing so, some indication of the effects of aggregation may be discerned.

Perhaps the minimum level of disaggregation is by the four major consuming sectors: residential, commercial, industrial, and transportation. The first three groups recognize the essential difference in the motivation for consumption. Residential demand for energy products is derived from consumer preferences on the basis of assumed behavior such as utility maximization, as distinguished from the demand for energy products for the contribution they make to production, which assumes profit maximization as a motive. In this sense, at least, there is a similarity in behavioral hypotheses for members within each sector. Ideally, fuel consumption for transportation should be disaggregated in a similar way, but the necessary data are not available. Instead, gasoline is generally identified with private demand for automobiles, while jet fuel and diesel fuel are associated with commercial transportation.

Even among the studies that separate fuels and consuming sectors, as evidenced by the review of studies below, there are marked differences in price elasticities derived from samples that combine large groups of consuming units compared with samples at a finer level of aggregation. It is expected that more aggregative samples will in general exhibit greater price responsiveness than less aggregative samples, because the former provide greater opportunity for systematic variation in consumption behavior that is correlated with, yet unrelated to, price variation.

The majority of demand studies use national or statewide aggregates as the unit of observation. Cross-state observations are useful because the model can then pick up the influence of climatic and demographic differences by geographic area. In addition, cross-state differences in fuel prices and incomes are often needed to increase variation in sample data because time-series variation is inadequate for most periods before 1973. However, the cross-sectional results are subject to misinterpretation. Price elasticities obtained from state variations in the data, for example, are strictly relevant only with respect to changes in relative state prices. Persistent differences in fuel prices across states lead to significant differences in energy consumption patterns. It is more economical to use electricity for residential space heating in some states, fuel oil in others, coal in others, and natural gas in still others because of price differences. More important, the location of business by states is dependent on relative energy costs, with energy-intensive industries tending to locate where their fuel needs may be obtained at the lowest cost. One should not expect a nationwide increase in the price of a fuel, keeping relative state prices constant, to produce the same effect on consumption patterns as that reflected in a comparison of a lower with a higher cost state. In fact, we would expect these differences across states to lead to overestimates of fuel price elasticities.

The data at different levels of aggregation differ by fuel and consuming sector. The greatest variety is found in residential electricity consumption, where, in addition to national and state observations, data exist for utility district, city, and households. Two household surveys of residential natural gas consumption have been used, and one survey of commercial gas consumption. The latter represents the only breakdown of commercial fuel consumption by type of commercial establishment. In the industrial sector, data at the firm level exist only for electric power generation. Fuel consumption in manufacturing is available at the state or national level for total manufacturing and for two-digit and three-digit Standard Industrial Classification (SIC) categories. Records of transportation fuel consumption are maintained at the state or national level only, and distinguish among sales by product category without regard to consuming sector or type of use. Census data on automobile ownership has been used in at least one gasoline demand study, however.

There are substantial differences in the quality of data regularly maintained by type of energy product. The most accurate and complete information is available for electricity consumption, because of data reporting requirements established for public utilities. But even here serious measurement problems arise. Consuming sectors are defined in the data by the rate structure paid by users. Residential users pay residential rates, commercial users pay commercial rates, and industrial users pay industrial rates. However, consumers in one sector may pay rates identified with another sector, depending on the level of consumption. In addition, some categories are established by arbitrary definitions. For example, individually metered dwellings and gang-metered buildings with fewer than five households are typically classified as residential, while sales to buildings with more than five households are classified as commercial. The basic information is supplied by individual utilities and, to make matters worse, the definition of class varies from utility to utility.

The most serious information gaps are in the area of petroleum products, where, as noted for transportation fuels, systematic records are kept of sales by product only, with no distinction by consuming sector or type of use. Gasoline sales are not distinguished by automobile versus other purposes, or by private versus commercial consumption. Fuel oil sales do not distinguish residential space heating from commercial and industrial uses. It is usually assumed that the consumption of specific petroleum products may be identified with specific consumer markets, such as gasoline with private automobiles, lighter grade distillates with residential consumption, and heavier fuel oils with commercial or industrial consumption. The only systematic records of fuel oil consumption by sector are those obtained from surveys of manufacturers on the amounts and values of fuels as burned, and from similar records for public utilities.

The importance of these measurement and aggregation errors in the analysis of demand elasticities is a matter of speculation that can be evaluated only by a comparison of results obtained from different samples, collected from different sources and at various levels of aggregation. Thus, in the survey of studies that follows, characteristics of the unit of observation become another important criterion in the review and evaluation of demand studies. Of central concern in this comparison, as in the comparison of analytical approaches, is whether the pattern of demand elasticity estimates is related to the type of data employed.

The Identification Problem

Any statistical analysis of supply or demand is confronted with the general problem of identification.[11] To paraphrase Schultz (1938), the basic question is whether it is possible to deduce statistically the theoretical demand or supply functions when we know only the observations corresponding to the intersections of unknown demand and supply curves at different points in time or across different classes of consumers. Each observation on price and quantity corresponds to a point on both the supply curve and the demand curve, and the statistical problem is identifying a supply curve or a demand curve from a collection of such points.

If it were known that the demand relationship between price and quantity was stable and the supply relationship shifted from one unit of observation to another, the sample of data points would lie along the theoretical demand relation and it could be estimated with ease. Similarly, a theoretical supply relation would result if demand shifted along a stable supply curve. Unless the researcher has reason to believe one or the other behaves as described, the statistical analysis must proceed as if the observations reflect shifts in both relations. Otherwise, what is supposed to be an estimated demand curve, containing parameters that reflect the effect of prices and other variables on consumption, is a hybrid of both supply and demand, with parameters that have no economic meaning. Even when the identification problem is recognized and properly handled, an estimation problem remains. Available estimation techniques have

[11]For a thorough discussion, see Fisher (1966).

desirable properties only with respect to large samples, so that a problem of small sample bias and inefficiency remains. In addition, some techniques are not robust in the presence of specification errors, so that parameter estimates may be subject to large errors in certain applications.

The identification problem arises because there are two or more variables that are causally interdependent in the same equation and whose values are therefore determined simultaneously. In a demand equation quantity and price are simultaneously determined if price affects quantity demanded and quantity demanded also affects the price. Price and quantity would not be interdependent if we could assume, for example, that supply were perfectly elastic. In this case price determines the point of consumption along the demand curve, but shifts in demand do not affect the price. The direction of causation flows from price to quantity, but not the reverse.

The assumption of perfectly elastic supply is most frequently employed in the literature on energy demand in order to free the analysis from the complications of supply considerations. It is an assumption that is in general questionable and, indeed, in some fuel markets, is almost certainly invalid. Moreover, the assumption is incomplete when interpreted only with regard to supply conditions for the fuel in question. Because energy products are consumed in association with energy-using equipment, supply conditions for fuel-specific equipment are potentially as important as supply conditions for the fuel itself. The assumption of perfectly elastic supply must be interpreted to include the relevant durable goods as well as the fuel. This assumption is also questionable and, as discussed below, in some cases is obviously incorrect.

The nature of the interaction between supply and demand gives rise to another general problem of identifying demand relations for energy products. The common assumption underlying demand analysis is that markets are able to achieve an equilibrium through adjustments in prices: excess demand leads to an increase in price that will close the gap between supply and demand, while excess supply causes a reduction in price that will clear the market. The equilibrium condition is required to assume that observations on price and quantity do in fact lie along a theoretical demand curve. However, government regulations have at different times and to varying degrees interrupted this normal equilibrating function of prices in virtually every fuel market.

The following sections describe these identification problems as they arise in energy product markets and discuss the techniques frequently used in the literature to address them.

Interdependence of fuel prices and quantities

The markets for electricity and natural gas provide clear examples of the interdependence between price and quantity because customers do not face a single price but a rate schedule, where the unit price declines in discrete steps as consumption increases. A two-way causal relationship is established in which quantity consumed is dependent on the price schedule and location on the price schedule is dependent on quantity consumed. Two problems arise: how to model the interrelationship between price and quantity and, because there is a schedule of prices instead of a single price, how to represent price in the model. The first problem is the usual identification problem in that supply considerations determine the downward-sloping rate schedule. The second problem is a matter of correctly specifying the price consumers respond to.

A common view starting with Houthakker (1951) is that the marginal price is relevant in the demand equation because the consumer achieves equilibrium by equating costs and utility at the margin. However, as noted by Taylor (1977), the "marginal price is relevant to a consumer's decision only when he is consuming in the block to which it attaches; it governs behavior while the consumer is in that block, but it does not, in and of itself, determine why he consumes in that block as opposed to some other block."[12] Taylor demonstrates that consumers may react to changes in fixed charges or to an intramarginal rate, even though the marginal rate remains unchanged, and differentially to changes in the marginal rate depending on what happens to fixed charges and intramarginal rates. Thus, he concludes "the marginal price must be included in the demand function, as well as a quantity that measures the impact of the customer charge and intramarginal prices."[13]

Taylor's analysis represents a technically correct application of conventional utility-maximizing theory for an individual consumer, but the analysis does not solve the problem. To begin with, a

[12]Taylor (1977), p. 70.
[13]Ibid., p. 73.

multiple-rate price schedule implies a kinked budget constraint, where the kinks correspond to jumps in the rate schedule. While a conventional demand schedule may be constructed for each continuous segment of the budget constraint, the overall demand schedule will be multivalued, with more than one equilibrium quantity consistent with each price. Taylor, Blattenberger, and Verleger (1977) demonstrate that the discontinuity problem is mitigated when aggregating across households at the market level since the relationship between average household consumption and the average price will approach a continuous function as the number of households increases, provided tastes and income vary across households. However, as noted in the last section, aggregation across heterogeneous households creates other bias problems. Moreover, average consumption has a questionable operational interpretation when it is obtained over households with different incomes and different demographic characteristics. Finally, because individuals will be consuming within different rate blocks, it is difficult to associate an appropriate "average" rate schedule with average consumption.

Theoretical arguments notwithstanding, the issue ultimately requires an acceptable practical interpretation. For example, it is unlikely that most customers are aware of the marginal price for each increment of consumption, and therefore they cannot be expected to base their consumption expenditures accordingly. The use of an average price based on actual consumption expenditures is unlikely to be a correct specification either, because it is a figure that can be calculated only after the fact. On the other hand, marginal prices and average prices may serve as adequate surrogates for the true measure. It is conceivable, for example, that consumers are influenced by some notion of an expected price that behaves much like an average price.

The important consideration for forecasting is the bias that will be imparted to estimated price elasticities if the correct specification is not used, but it is not known whether the correct specification is best represented by a measure of the marginal price, the average price, or the entire rate structure. This is essentially an empirical question that no amount of theorizing can establish; all that can be said is that an incorrect specification will produce biased estimates. Taylor (1975) has argued that the bias is similar to that resulting from an omitted variable when the appropriate specification requires more than a single measure such as a marginal or an average price. To the extent that the omitted component is positively correlated with the price variable, there will be a positive covariance between the price variable and the error term. The result would be a negative bias added to the expected value of the estimated price coefficient, which implies that the estimate will in general be too large. A positive bias would result if the omitted component were negatively correlated with the price variable.

Because the appropriate specification is unknown, and because the included price measure may be positively or negatively correlated with the omitted variable, one cannot conclude whether the bias will be positive or negative. Furthermore, a determination of the nature of the bias depends on the absence of any other specification errors in the estimating equation. If the equation is subject to aggregation errors, inappropriate functional form, other omitted variables, measurement errors, or a disturbance term that is not independently and identically distributed, the effect of an omitted price term becomes uncertain.

What we are left with is another uncertain situation that cannot be resolved on the basis of deductive reasoning alone. What we can do, in an effort to evaluate the importance of the price issue and its apparent impact on empirical results, is compare the results of different studies that utilize different measures of price in the demand equations. Essentially three alternative measures have been employed: average prices, marginal prices, and representatives of the entire rate schedule.

Average price specifications.   Among the average price specifications, the most common uses an *ex post* measure of average revenues paid by a group of customers, calculated by dividing total expenditures of the group by the quantity consumed. An alternative approach suggested by Halvorsen (1978) is to estimate the slope of actual rate schedules with a log-linear price function, and use estimated values of price in the demand equation for electricity. The price function is estimated using average price data associated with corresponding consumption levels. Halvorsen demonstrates that this procedure will not bias price elasticities of demand, if the linear representation is valid, because the use of average price data rather than marginal prices only affects the intercept term and the intercept term (because it is constant) does not affect the price elasticity coefficient.

Halvorsen's argument, to the extent it is valid, means that it makes little difference whether average or marginal prices are used to calculate estimated prices, but the argument does not resolve the issue of whether more than one characteristic of the rate schedule should be included. Each measure, by itself, conveys only part of the information contained in a rate schedule. In addition, Halvorsen's price equation averages across different blocks on the same rate schedule. The fitted price equation will approximate the characteristics of a family of rate schedules, and may have a slope which is flatter or steeper than any of the individual rate schedules used to obtain it. That is to say, the aggregate schedule may convey a price response quite different from that reflected by any of the individual components.

Marginal price specifications. Among the marginal price specifications, the most common measure is based on the difference between Typical Electric Bills (TEBs) at different levels of consumption.[14] This gives a measure of the change in per unit prices moving from one consumption block to another. Taylor, Blattenberger, and Verleger (1977) estimate a "typical" marginal price for residential consumption in each state, based on the marginal block that corresponds to average consumption in each utility district. The statewide measure is a weighted average of each district, using the proportion of state customers in the district as the weights. Acton, Mitchell, and Mowill (1976) use a similar procedure at a more disaggregated level, looking at the marginal block price corresponding to average consumption for households within small subdivisions of Los Angeles County. The household survey data used by McFadden, Puig, and Kirshner (1977) for electricity, and by Olsen, Robeson, and Neri (1979) for natural gas, achieve the finest level of aggregation. With each customer's fuel bill they associate an actual measure of the average price paid and the applicable marginal block rate.

A few studies attempt to capture more than one characteristic of the price structure. Taylor, Blattenberger, and Verleger (1977) include with their marginal price variable a measure of the fixed charge for residential electricity consumption, calculated by the difference between total expenditures (in each state) and the amount that would have been spent if the marginal block rate applied to all consumption. McFadden, Puig, and Kirshner (1977) use in addition to marginal and

[14]Typical electric bills are found in U.S. Federal Power Commission, *Typical Electric Bills* (Washington, D.C., Government Printing Office), various years.

average price measures a variable designed to reflect the rate of decline of the marginal price, defined as the difference between TEBs at 750 and 1000 kWh of consumption divided by the difference between TEBs at 500 and 750 kWh consumption.

The review of electricity and natural gas demand studies that follows will be organized to facilitate comparisons among results obtained with different price measures. These comparisons are useful because, as noted above, the direction and importance of any bias that results from different price specifications requires empirical verification. The specification of the price variable thus becomes another basis for comparing empirical demand studies.

The identification problem.   We now return to the first problem listed at the beginning of this section—the general identification problem that arises from an interdependence between price and quantity. This problem is more general than that associated with declining rate schedules because, first, it applies to all fuel products and, second, it remains to be considered regardless of the specific measure of price employed. The use of any *ex post* measure of price at a point of consumption fails to take into account the possible influence of quantity on that price measure. We have noted that both marginal and average prices for electricity and natural gas will decline at higher consumption levels. Thus, an increase in consumption that is unrelated to a price change will cause average or marginal prices to fall, which in turn will cause a further increase in consumption. The first step will nevertheless appear in the data as a price effect, and, unless identified and separated from the second step, will add to the apparent price elasticity of demand and yield an overestimate of the true magnitude.

For petroleum products and coal, where supply prices may rise with higher levels of output, an increase in consumption may cause an increase in the supply price, which in turn will cause a reduction in the quantity of consumption. Again, the supply effect on price may be confused with the price effect on consumption, giving a biased measure of the true price elasticity of demand. The effect of supply can be ignored only if it is perfectly elastic; that is, only if the supply price does not change with quantity.

Many demand studies ignore the problem of separating supply and demand effects or simply pass over the problem with a warning that price elasticity estimates may be biased as a result. Other studies attempt to rationalize the use of single equation (one-way causation) models because of special characteristics of supply, and still others attempt to address the problem directly. The use of a single equation demand model for electricity or natural gas has been justified on the grounds that rate structures are regulated by public utility commissions, so the price cannot be considered a truly endogenous variable, as in a competitive market situation. At least the bias would not be as serious as in other commodity markets because regulators are unable to adjust price schedules immediately because costs are affected by volume. There is a time lag that, at least in the short run, breaks the connection between quantity and price.

A second argument is based on the nature of supply of primary fuels and their products. The supply of crude oil, natural gas, and coal depends primarily on a long history of past prices and will be only marginally affected by changes in current prices. In addition, as the argument goes, the supply process requires heavy capital investment and long lead times, implying that production plans are geared toward future as well as current consumption levels. At any point in time there will exist a positive level of unused capacity that may fluctuate to accommodate changes in consumption without corresponding fluctuations in prices. Again, the argument suggests that, in the short run at least, supply may be perfectly elastic.

Finally, Balestra (1967) argues in connection with residential supplies of natural gas that the existence of interruptible contracts, and the regulatory requirement for supplying residential consumption first, imply that changes in residential demand can be satisfied without changes in the price and without an interruption in service. This is again a short-run argument, and it applies only to changes in consumption with regard to existing gas customers. Moratoriums on new hookups in most states in the recent past illustrate the importance of supply conditions with regard to new gas demand.

These arguments apply primarily to short-run residential demand for electricity and natural gas. They are less valid for commercial and industrial demands, even in the short run, because customers are large enough to bargain with utilities, where prices, volumes, and interruptibility of service are all interdependent terms of the contract. They are also less valid with respect to petroleum products because the industry is highly sensitive to even small changes in normal inventory positions. It is concluded, therefore, that the analysis of energy demand must be sensitive to the implications associated with an interdependence between price and quantity.

In one of the earliest attempts to adjust for the problem, Fisher and Kaysen (1962) used first differences of average real prices to reduce the dependence of price on quantity in residential electricity demand. They argue that the effect of consumption on deflated average prices will be small because nominal rate schedules remained relatively stable compared with real prices during their sample period (1946–57). In addition, the use of first differences in real prices reduces any correlation between real and nominal prices. This procedure may be adequate when nominal rates are fairly stable and when analyzing short-run demand, but is inappropriate over periods of large price changes or across consumer groups facing significantly different rate schedules.

The traditional, and more general, approach to the problem is to treat price as an endogenous variable in the demand model. Price is estimated separately on the basis of cost considerations, and the estimated values are utilized in the demand equation in place of actual values to estimate price elasticities. The instrumental variables approach, as it is commonly referred to, breaks the correlation between the price variable and the error term in the demand equation, removing the systematic source of bias in estimating the price parameter. The estimators are not unbiased for small samples, but are consistent and fairly robust in the presence of specification errors. This technique is used occasionally in electricity demand models and infrequently in natural gas demand models or in the demand for gasoline. Otherwise, demand analysis is conducted under the implicit or explicit assumption of a perfectly elastic supply. Treatment of the identification problem is therefore another criterion for comparing and evaluating different demand studies.

The supply of fuel-using equipment

Characteristics of the supply of fuel-using equipment are similar in effect to those just discussed for supply of fuels since fuels are consumed in association with equipment. These include the household appliances and industrial motors that use electricity, the furnaces and boilers that use natural gas and fuel oil, and the automobiles that use gasoline. The consumption of each fuel is dependent on its availability and price. In addition, the price and availability of fuel-using equipment is determined in part by the quantity of equipment demanded, which is in turn dependent upon the quantity of fuels demanded.

There is, in other words, an identification problem in demand estimation that is associated with the supply of equipment in much the same way as that associated with the supply of fuels. The problem can be ignored only if the supply of equipment is perfectly elastic. Otherwise, an increase in fuel demand will alter the price of equipment, and in turn alter the demand for fuels. The two-way dependence of fuel consumption and equipment prices must be separated in order to focus on the demand effect alone. To illustrate, suppose the supply of gas-fired furnaces is substantially more elastic than that of oil-fired furnaces. A reduction in the relative price of oil may be expected to lead to a substitution of oil furnaces for gas furnaces, but the shift in demand will drive up the price of oil furnaces relative to gas furnaces. Unless this equipment price effect can be identified in the model, the measured price elasticity of demand for oil will be understated.

It appears that the problem can be handled by including equipment prices in the fuel demand models. However, there are drawbacks. First, information on equipment prices is scarce and of poor quality. Second, if equipment prices are affected by the quantity of fuel consumed, there will be a correlation between the error term in the fuel demand equation and the price variable that will cause biased and inconsistent estimates of the parameters of the demand equation. This is important in long-run fuel demand models, where changes in capital stocks are important, and where equipment supplies are fairly inelastic. Consistent estimates may be obtained using the instrumental variables approach described above, with estimates of prices substituted for actual values. This requires a separate model and data for determining equipment prices.

Third, the problem of identifying the effect of equipment supply is complicated. For example, until recently, imported models provided the only viable small car option for American customers. The range of choice was small, service and repair were inconvenient, and rising import prices and psychological factors slowed penetration in U.S. markets. Nevertheless, penetration increased steadily over time while domestic manufacturers failed to provide competitive domestic options. Not until 1979, when the shift in preferences toward smaller cars became massive and unquestionably permanent did domestic manufacturers begin to move assertively into the small car market. The initial reluctance to reduce the size and weight of new car fleets to meet federal fuel-efficiency standards suddenly vanished and manufacturers began to exceed the minimum standards. But the supply process has been slow and nearly disastrous for two of the three major auto companies.

The price responsiveness of gasoline consumption has been reduced by the limited availability of fuel-efficient cars. New car purchases have not matched desired demand, and the stock of autos has not adjusted as rapidly to changes in gasoline prices as a consequence. The lag in adjustment is not fully explained by incomplete adjustments in desired demand, nor increasing costs of fuel-efficient cars, although both forces have been at work. The effect is to reduce, or stretch out, the apparent long-term price elasticity of demand for gasoline. Because supply, not demand, considerations are responsible for this effect, they must be identified and accounted for in order to derive an accurate measure of the true demand response.

None of the fuel demand studies available to date has attempted to separate the influence of equipment supplies, nor have any discussed the implications of this omission for their results. While this is not a serious omission in many fuel markets, it can be important in certain cases. In these cases, characteristics of equipment supplies should be treated as endogenous variables in the fuel demand model, following an approach similar to that for fuel supplies where fuel prices are treated as endogenous variables.

Disequilibrium markets

Another variation of the identification problem arises when prices for some fuels do not serve their market-clearing function. In this event, prices may not record equilibrium points on behavioral supply or demand curves, making it difficult if not impossible to infer from observable data the true characteristics of unrestricted behavioral relationships. Furthermore, models based on, or deduced from, equilibrium market conditions are not appropriate.

In the case of natural gas, price controls on interstate sales since 1954 have interfered with long-run market equilibrium. The period before

1965 was characterized by excess supply at the wellhead because pipelines were not completed and consumer markets could not be served. A regulated price was established that reflected market conditions at the time, but the price was not consistent with long-run market equilibrium. After 1965, demand exceeded the rate of reserve replacement, and a supply shortage gradually developed that led to interruptions of service to commercial and industrial customers. By 1970, potential new gas customers were not allowed hookups in many areas. Thus, before 1965 demand could not be satisfied because supply was inaccessible, while afterwards demand could not be satisfied at market prices because of supply shortages. In both cases, price and quantity consumed would not reflect the true demand for natural gas because of supply constraints. Market price was not allowed to close the gap between supply and demand.

The modeling literature has not yet explicitly handled the disequilibrium problem in the gas market. Balestra (1967) has given arguments to justify an equilibrium approach for modeling residential demand in the period before 1965, but they are questionable because the distribution system was incomplete. Even if an equilibrium approach is valid for the earlier period, the structure of the market has changed considerably over the years, so that neither the results nor the method seem appropriate for forecasting purposes. There also remains the problem of estimating commercial and industrial demand.

In the market for coal, demand was affected by the introduction of air pollution regulations beginning in 1967. As a result, this date marks an important change in the responsiveness of consumption to changes in the relative price of coal. The problem for modeling demand is more serious than a one-time structural shift caused by an institutional development. The impact of the clean air regulations is developing over time, with different implications for new and existing firms and with varying restrictions by geographical location. In some cases air pollution control equipment is installed, in other cases operations are shut down, and in still other cases no changes are required. New operations face site limitations and licensing delays, as well as added capital costs.

The regulations have contributed to a large disparity between the price for Btu of coal and other fuels compared with the preregulation period. The disparity means that existing coal-fired plants have a large fuel cost advantage compared with alternatives and that large increases in the relative price of coal will not reverse the advantage.

Existing coal-fired plants will tend to operate to capacity and will be unaffected by major swings in relative fuel prices. Short-term demand will not be price responsive. Long-term demand will not be fully responsive either, because of delays and impediments to new investment. The fuel cost advantage of coal reflects more than a simple internalization of the cost of air pollution control devices because the costs involve more than pollution control equipment and because these costs have not yet become well defined and stable. The demand for coal remains in a state of disequilibrium because the institutional constraints are still in disequilibrium.

The literature on coal demand is no further developed than that for natural gas. As yet, econometric models of coal demand that recognize the institutional problems do no more than restrict sample observations to periods before 1967. The usefulness of the estimates for subsequent periods is therefore highly questionable.

Finally, mention should be made of disequilibrium periods in the market for petroleum products. Following the implementation of price controls in 1971, the allocation of petroleum products became increasingly subject to government regulation. Price controls were accompanied by profit controls, cost-pass-through regulations, allocation priorities, and mandatory wedding of buyers and sellers at each stage in the supply process from crude oil acquisition to retail sales. Some of the distortions produced by these controls have been obvious. Prices moved in discrete jumps, as the rules allowed, rather than as market conditions would dictate. Spot shortages by fuel and region were handled with adjustments in allocation rules because prices could not adjust to perform the market-clearing function. General shortages of gasoline were met with a combination of price increases and implicit rationing measures. While these controls have not been as rigid and well structured as those in coal and natural gas markets, there are the same concerns about forecasting petroleum demand based on observations drawn from a different institutional environment.

Functional Forms and Related Estimation Problems

Another issue that must be confronted by all econometric demand studies is the choice of functional form of the estimating equation. The choice is important because of the implications about the nature of elasticities, and because alternative forms will interact with the data to affect the results. The oldest and most common approach is to specify quantities demanded as a double logarithmic function of the relevant arguments, i.e.,

$$\log Q \ = \ a \ + \ b \log P \ + \ c \log Y \ + \ d \log Z \qquad\qquad (2\text{-}24)$$

where Q is the quantity demanded, P is its price, Y is income in the case of final consumption or output in the case of intermediate demand, and Z is a vector of other variables. Prices and income are usually measured relative to an index of all prices, in keeping with the theory of demand that real income and relative prices are the relevant variables. For most goods, it may be assumed that demand is more sensitive to their own-prices than to the prices of other goods, so attention is focused on own-price elasticities. Among energy products, there is considerable room for interfuel substitution, so competing fuel prices are often entered as arguments and, in some cases, quantity is expressed in terms of the market share of total energy consumption.

The form of equation (2-24) is convenient because it gives elasticities directly as coefficients: estimates of b and c are, respectively, measures of price and income elasticities. However, the form of equation (2-24) may not be consistent with demand theory. If c is greater than 1, the equation implies that the budget share of the good in question would increase without limit as real income rises. For income-elastic goods, in other words, the use of a model for prediction will eventually lead to gross overestimates. The model implies in addition that the elasticities will remain constant over any range of values the explanatory variables take on, contrary to what we should expect from theory and intuition. One would normally expect the price elasticity to eventually fall with rising income as the fraction of the budget devoted to consumption of this good becomes less important. Furthermore, changes in exogenous variables produce changes in the volume of consumption, which are equivalent to a shift in demand relative to the price variable and, except under special conditions, will cause a change in the price elasticity. For example, an increase in income at constant prices will increase demand and, for any absolute change in quantity associated with a change in price, the percentage change in quantity will fall, thus reducing the measure of price elasticity.

Mount, Chapman, and Tyrrell (1973) try a variable elasticity version obtained by adding to (2-24) the inverses of each explanatory variable as new arguments, i.e.,

$$e\frac{1}{P} + f\frac{1}{Y} + g\frac{1}{Z} \tag{2-25}$$

where e, f, and g are parameters. The own-price elasticity would be given by

$$(b - e/P) \tag{2-26}$$

and would vary with the price level. If $e < 0$, the price elasticity would increase with P, but at a decreasing rate. Similarly, if $f > 0$, the income elasticity would rise as income rises. Elasticity estimates using the constant and variable elasticity versions are reported in the next chapter.

Another question of interpretation of the estimated elasticities concerns their symmetry: that is, whether the same elasticity holds for price increases as well as price decreases. The static theory of demand suggests that the adjustments would be symmetric, but in a dynamic world they need not be because time lags will differ. It is in general more difficult to adjust to less of a given commodity as required by a price increase than it is to adjust to more as permitted by a price decrease. The stock of fuel-using equipment adjusts to a consumption pattern consistent with relative prices, but the capital stock cannot be easily replaced as relative prices change. Moreover, tastes change with the capital stock; for example, air conditioners are regarded as luxuries before they are experienced and necessities afterwards. For similar reasons, more rapid changes in prices should not be expected to produce the same demand response as gradual changes. We might expect the lag in the adjustment process to shorten with the rapidity of price changes, but it is unlikely that a doubling of prices that occurs within a month will produce the same effect on consumption as a doubling over several years.

The characteristics imposed on the elasticities follow from the behavioral restrictions maintained by the form of the equation. The form (2-24) is consistent with utility maximization only if the utility function is linear logarithmic, and consistent with profit maximization of firms only if the production function is log linear.[15] The first case requires that elasticities of substitution in consumption among all pairs of commodities be constant and equal, and the second case requires that elasticities of substitution among inputs in production be constant and equal. It is often thought that these restrictions will not unduly affect estimates of price and income elasticities. However, Deaton (1974) has shown that models based on additive preferences (or production functions) enforce an approximate linear relationship between income (or output) and price elasticities that, as a result, may permit the independent measurement of only one elasticity per commodity.

The restrictions implied by the model, in other words, may be more stringent than necessary or desired. The assumed properties may hold, but it is often the case that their existence should be a result of the empirical analysis rather than a starting point in a model which presumes it. The model (2-24) is a convenient and useful means of summarizing the evidence from a given sample, but care should be exercised in interpreting the results.

An alternative to (2-24) with as yet comparatively few applications is one of the so-called flexible functional forms that impose fewer restrictions on underlying utility functions or production functions as part of the maintained hypotheses. The most common flexible functional form used in energy demand analysis is the translog function developed by Christensen, Jorgenson, and Lau (1973, 1975). For utility-based consumer analysis, this approach specifies a quadratic logarithmic approximation of utility functions that allows expenditure shares to vary with total expenditures and where substitution patterns among pairs of commodities are not constant and equal. On the production side, the translog specifies a second-order approximation to any production frontier that permits more flexible patterns of substitution and transformation than models specifying constant elasticities of substitution in production.

These functional forms are used in conjunction with duality theory to yield systems of consumer demand functions and input demand functions in terms of relative prices only, although scale variables are sometimes added. The models are not easily modified to incorporate additional determinants that might be relevant in disaggregated

[15]See Christensen, Jorgenson, and Lau (1973, 1975).

demand analysis, as the number of parameters to be estimated increases exponentially. This disadvantage is particularly troublesome in models with more than one endogenous variable, because the estimation process becomes intractable. Consequently, all of the applications of this technique reviewed below assume that fuel prices and final outputs are exogenous. Furthermore, the models have been employed in static form only, because the addition of a lag adjustment process creates internal inconsistencies. Kuh (1976) argues that lagged adjustment processes are inconsistent with the static properties of constant returns to scale, symmetry, and convexity, which are required in order to reduce the number of parameters that must be estimated. Similarly, Berndt, Fuss, and Waverman (1977) show that the incorporation of lag processes can produce short-run price elasticities of demand that exceed long-run elasticities; that factor demands may not be capable of yielding output levels actually produced; and that cost shares may be in equilibrium while input levels are out of equilibrium.

Applications of the translog approach to energy demand have concentrated on production sectors rather than the household sector. The work of Atkinson and Halvorsen (1976b) on interfuel substitution in electric power generation and manufacturing will serve to illustrate the technique. Starting with the unit cost function for the jth industry in equation (2-16) above, recall

$$V = V(P_e, P_o, P_g, P_c)$$

where the arguments refer to prices of electricity, oil, gas and coal, respectively. A translog functional form for the unit cost function is written as

$$\ln V = a + \Sigma\alpha_i \ln P_i + 0.5 \underset{i\,j}{\Sigma\Sigma} \gamma_{ij} \ln P_i \ln P_j \text{ for } i,j = e, o, g, c$$
(2-28)

Logarithmic derivatives of (2-28) with respect to each fuel price give their respective cost shares, which sum to unity. In addition, the form of (2-28) is restricted so that the share parameter estimated in different fuel share equations takes on the same value; that is, cross-price parameters are symmetric. Finally, because the cost shares sum to unity, one equation must be deleted to avoid singularity in the covariance matrix, and the parameters of the omitted equation are derived from the remaining parameters in the model. The estimating equation for the cost shares becomes:

$$M_i = \alpha_i + \sum_j \gamma_{ij} (\ln p_j - \ln p_i) + u_i \quad \text{for } i = e, o, g;$$

$$j = e, o, g, c; \; i \neq j \tag{2-29}$$

From estimates of the parameters in (2-29), price elasticities may be derived using the following formulas[16] for own-price elasticities by:

$$E_{ii} = \frac{\alpha_i^2 - \alpha_i + \gamma_{ii}}{\alpha_i}, \quad i = e, o, g, c \tag{2-30}$$

and for cross-price elasticities by

$$E_{ij} = \frac{\alpha_i \alpha_j + \gamma_{ij}}{\alpha_i}, \quad i, j = e, o, g, c \tag{2-31}$$

Because (2-30) and (2-31) are obtained from unit cost functions, they are to be interpreted under the condition that total energy input remains constant.

The unit cost function is used when data are not available on nonenergy inputs and the price of output. The necessary assumptions are rather stringent, however, as noted above. When this information is available, as in the case of electric power generation, Atkinson and Halvorsen (1976b) use a restricted profit function specified as

$$\Pi = \Pi(P_c, P_o, P_g, Z_K, Z_L, Z_T) \tag{2-32}$$

where Π is normalized restricted profits of conventional steam electric power plants; P_c, P_o and P_g are normalized prices of coal, oil, and gas, respectively; Z_K and Z_L are inputs of capital and labor; and Z_T is the vintage of capital. Normalization is achieved by dividing profits and prices of variable inputs by the price of output. Capital and labor are treated as fixed inputs to avoid estimation problems. Halvorsen (1978)

[16]See Halvorsen (1978).

regards this assumption as unimportant, but his interpretation is questionable in view of the importance of factor substitution in long-run fuel demands. The vintage of capital is included to account for different technologies across different plants.

The translog representation of (2-32) is given by

$$\ln \Pi = a + \sum_i \alpha_i P_i + 0.5 \sum_i \sum_j \gamma_{ih} \ln P_i \ln P_h$$

$$+ \sum_i \sum_j \delta_{ij} \ln P_i \ln Z_j + \sum \beta_j \ln Z_j$$

$$+ 0.5 \sum_j \sum_k \phi_{jk} \ln Z_j \ln Z_k; \quad i, h = c, o, g; \quad j, k = K, L, T$$

$$(2\text{-}33)$$

and demand equations for each fuel are given by

$$- \frac{\partial \ln \Pi}{\partial \ln P_i} = M_i = - \left(\alpha_i + \sum_h \gamma_{ih} \ln P_h + \sum_j \delta_{ij} \ln Z_j \right)$$

$$i, h = c, o, g; \quad j = K, L, T \tag{2-34}$$

where M_i is the ratio of normalized expenditures on fuel i to normalized restricted profit. Cross-equation equality restrictions and symmetry conditions are imposed on the Y_{ij} in the same fashion as in (2-28). Own-price and cross-price elasticities, calculated at sample means, are obtained from (2-34) in the same way as (2-30) and (2-31).

The translog approach, to conclude, has the advantage of deriving fuel demand functions explicitly from theoretical formulations, with greater generality as to the maintained hypotheses underlying consumer and firm behavior. However, the procedure requires a number of other restrictions and assumptions in order to become tractable for estimation. A certain amount of arbitrariness is involved regardless of the approach taken.

In addition to the drawbacks mentioned earlier, three additional characteristics of translog estimators deserve mention. First, a convexity condition is often imposed on the demand equations, which precludes the possibility of upward-sloping demand functions. As Kuh (1976) points out, if the results of an unconstrained relation are not consistent with convexity, something is seriously wrong in the model or the data and the inconsistency should not be expunged by assumption. Second, there is reason to believe that translog estimates may be more unstable than those obtained with other functional forms. The source of this difference is the second-order approximation of an unknown utility function or production function, based on a Taylor series expansion. This representation is appropriate for small changes in cost shares and relative prices, such as those associated with sample periods before 1973, but may be unstable and misleading for forecasting events since 1973. Finally, the translog elasticities will tend to look good even when the component parameter estimates perform poorly. For example, the own-price elasticity in equation (2-30) may be written as $M_i - 1 + \gamma_{ii}/M_i$, where M_i lies between zero and unity, so the elasticities will appear to be plausible even when the estimated values of γ_{ii} are zero.

Separating Influences Acting on Demand

Implied in many of the issues discussed so far is a problem of separating the various influences that act upon demand. Specifically, there is a problem of separating the influence of price from the influence of other determinants of demand. The problem arises at three levels: the data, the structure of the model, and the underlying behavioral process. Each has been discussed above, so a summary will suffice here.

Starting with the data, there is first the problem of identifying a price effect from a sample period characterized by little variation in relative fuel prices. This problem is often addressed by pooling time-series and cross-section data, but this introduces cross-sectional factors that must be identified and accounted for. In many cases, several influences move together with prices, cross-sectionally or over time, making it difficult or impossible to separate individual influences. In addition, the data refer to *ex post* market transactions which combine the influence of supply and demand after adjustments have been made. Finally, the more aggregative the data, the more they combine separate events that operate at different intensities and in different directions.

The structure of the model imposes its own restrictions on the estimated parameters and defines the possible relationships that may be revealed from the data. The simpler and more compact the model, the fewer details may be extracted from the data about the demand process. Static models cannot provide information about the adjustment process over time. Single-equation, aggregate consumption models cannot reveal details underlying capital stock adjustments, interfuel substitution, or interfactor substitution. And, the form of the estimating equation imposes restrictions on the behavioral parameters of the model because of assumptions about consumer or firm behavior, because of direct restrictions on the estimated values, or because of assumptions about the marketplace.

The third category refers mainly to dynamic interrelationships among the components of demand as implied by the behavioral process. The interrelationship between fuel prices and income in residential demand behavior will serve to illustrate the problem. First, relative prices and income jointly determine the initial fuel choice decision. Second, price changes and income affect the rate of utilization of existing fuel-using equipment. There is also a scale effect on fuel consumption determined by income-related variables, such as appliance saturation, size of the house, and number of cars. But these characteristics of the capital stock are determined in part by relative fuel prices as well. Thus, income and prices affect fuel consumption directly, but also affect a number of other variables that in turn influence fuel consumption. It is difficult to separate the direct and indirect effects of income and prices and identify their influence relative to the contribution of other factors. To do so requires a comprehensive and detailed model of the elements of demand and a sample of data rich enough to apply the model. This level of detail is seldom possible in practice.

Concluding Remark

This chapter has reviewed a number of issues that confront any econometric study of demand and some that have special interpretations when applied to energy products. As indicated, often it is not possible to deduce with reasonable certainty the magnitude or direction of the effect of those issues on estimated elasticities. For this reason, it is fortunate that the literature on energy demand has approached these questions in a variety of ways. What may otherwise seem to be a profusion of alternative estimates provides a means for evaluating the sensitivity of elasticity estimates to the problems encountered and the approaches taken. The chapters that follow are organized to facilitate these comparisons.

chapter 3

Demand for Electricity

It is appropriate to begin an analysis of the empirical demand literature with electricity because the variety of modeling efforts and the quality of the data far exceed those available for other energy products. As a result, it may be said that more is known about the characteristics of electricity demand than for any other energy product. Yet, even here, there is wide disagreement about the responsiveness of demand to changes in prices and incomes, and surprisingly broad gaps in the understanding of the nature of this process. Moreover, it will become evident from the review that follows that the understanding of electricity demand varies a great deal among consuming sectors.

In order to facilitate comparisons, the empirical demand studies are organized first by major consuming sector and then by estimation procedure. In keeping with the discussion in chapter 2, the studies are distinguished according to the type of model and data employed. A summary of research results is provided for each consuming sector.

Residential Electricity Demand

Twenty-five different studies of residential electricity demand are compared here, each of which may be distinguished in some detail (excluded from the comparison are time-of-day and seasonal demand studies). There are more than twenty-five sets of estimates since some of the studies contain more than one set, derived from different samples or different model specifications. Table 3-1 summarizes the major studies reviewed here, along with their corresponding estimates of price and income elasticities, organized according to the type of model and data used. Three groups of reduced-form models are distinguished—static consumption models, dynamic consumption models, and fuel shares models—and a group of structural demand models that separate appliance demands from appliance utilization rates. Each group is further categorized according to the use of aggregate or micro level data, and according to the measurement of electricity prices on a marginal or average basis. The features of each category have been discussed in chapter 2 and need not be repeated here. Overall, there are wide disparities among the estimates reported by different studies. To add to the confusion, some short-run estimates exceed (in absolute value) other long-run estimates. Price elasticities range from -0.03 to -0.54 in the short run and from -0.45 to -2.20 in the long run. The overlap is even more confusing among the income elasticities, as both short-run and long-run estimates range from 0 to 2.0. It is little wonder that decision makers are reluctant to place great confidence in any specific values.

In order to make some sense out of the range of figures, observers frequently look for tendencies to cluster around specific values. The consensus value is then taken as the best point estimate of an elasticity. For example, if the outlying values in table 3-1 are excluded and one looks for tendencies to cluster around a specific figure, the consensus measure of the price elasticity would be around -0.2 in the short run and more than -1.0 in the long run. This procedure assumes, however, that the methods used to obtain the estimates are equally appropriate and that the values they give are equally reliable. This assumption is not correct, as we argue below, and it is frequently the case that estimates given by a minority of studies are the preferred ones.

The distribution of studies by type of model and data is not uniform, as indicated by table 3-1, and the most common approach is not the preferred one. The overwhelming majority of studies use reduced-form consumption models of either a static or dynamic specification. There are very few structural demand studies that attempt to separate appliance utilization rates from appliance saturation rates. And, there are only three separate studies that use micro level data. Several other

TABLE 3-1. SUMMARY OF ESTIMATED PRICE AND INCOME ELASTICITIES OF RESIDENTIAL DEMAND FOR ELECTRICITY BY TYPE OF MODEL AND DATA

Research study	Sample[a]	Price elasticity[b] Short-run	Price elasticity[b] Long-run	Income elasticity[b] Short-run	Income elasticity[b] Long-run
I. Reduced-Form Models					
A. Static consumption models					
1. Aggregate level data					
(a) Average prices					
Fisher, Kaysen (1962)	Time series: states, 1946–57	−0.16 to −0.24		0.07 to 0.33	
Moore (1970)	Cross-section: 407 utilities, 1963		−1.02		
Wilson (1971)	Cross-section: 77 cities, 1966		−1.33		n.s.
Anderson (1973)	Cross-section: states, 1960, 1970		−1.07		1.06
CRA (1976)	Pooled: states, 1966–72		−1.28		0.67
Halvorsen (1978)	Pooled: states, 1961–69		−1.20		0.48
			−1.14		0.52
(b) Marginal prices					
Lacy, Street (1975)	Times series: Alabama Power Co., 1967–74	−0.45		1.87	
Wills (1977)	Cross-section: Mass. utilities, 1975	−0.08		−0.32	
2. Disaggregated level data					
(a) Average prices: none					
(b) Marginal prices					
Halvorsen (1978)	Pooled: states, 1961–69		−1.53		0.72
McFadden, Puig (1975)	Pooled: states, 1961–69		−0.48		0.99
Acton, Mitchell, Mowill (1976)	Pooled: monthly, Los Angeles County, 1972–74		−0.70		0.40
Hewlett (1977)	Cross section: household survey, 1973 & 1975	−0.14		0.07	

continued

TABLE 3-1 *continued*

Research study	Sample[a]	Price elasticity[b]		Income elasticity[b]	
		Short-run	*Long-run*	*Short-run*	*Long-run*
B. Dynamic consumption models					
1. Aggregate level data					
(a) Average prices					
Houthakker, Taylor (1970)	Time series: U.S., 1946–64	−0.13	−1.89	0.13	1.94
Uri (1976)	Time series: monthly, U.S., 1971–75	−0.35		2.00	
Griffin (1974)	Time series: U.S., 1951–71	−0.06	−0.52	0.06	0.88
Mount, Chapman, Tyrrell (1973)	Pooled: states, 1946–70 (3 versions)	−0.14	−1.21	0.03	0.30
		−0.14	−1.20	0.02	0.20
		−0.36	−1.24	0.06	0.21
Gill, Maddala (1976)	Pooled: monthly, TVA area, 1962–67 and 1968–72	−0.49	−0.57	0.10	0.12
		−0.34	−0.62	0.12	0.22
Cohn, Hirst, Jackson (1977)	Pooled: states, 1951–74 and 1969–74	−0.14	−1.16	0.02	0.16
		−0.14	−0.47	0.16	0.56
(b) Marginal prices					
Houthakker, Verleger, Sheehan (1974)	Pooled: states, 1960–71 (3 prices)	−0.09	−1.19	0.13	1.63
		−0.03	−0.44	0.14	2.20
		−0.09	−1.02	0.14	1.64
Taylor, Blattenberger, Verleger (1977)	Pooled: states, 1956–72	−0.08	−0.82	0.10	1.08
2. Disaggregated level data					
(a) Average prices: none					
(b) Marginal prices					
Hewlett (1977)	Pooled: household survey, 1973 and 1975	−0.16	−0.45	n.s.	n.s.

C. Fuel shares models					
1. Static versions					
Chern (1976)	Pooled: states, 1971–72		−1.34		0.40
2. Dynamic versions					
Baughman, Joskow (1975)	Pooled: states, 1968–72	−0.19	−1.00	n.s.	n.s.
DOE (1978)	Pooled: regions, 1960–75	−0.18 to −0.54	−0.72 to −2.10	n.s.	n.s.
II. Structural Models					
A. Aggregate level data					
1. Average prices					
Fisher, Kaysen (1962)	Time series: states, 1946–57		n.s.		n.s.
Anderson (1973)	Cross-section: states, 1960 and 1970		−1.07		1.06
			−1.28		0.67
2. Marginal prices					
Taylor, Blattenberger, Verleger (1977)	Pooled: states, 1961–72	−0.16	−0.46	0.22	1.00
B. Disaggregated level data					
1. Average prices: none					
2. Marginal prices					
McFadden, Puig, Kirshner (1977)	Cross-section: household survey, 1975	−0.25	−0.66	0.21	0.39

[a] Observation periods are annual except where indicated otherwise.

[b] The estimates given are statistically significant at the 0.05 level. An entry of n.s. indicates not significant. A blank space means no estimate was attempted or reported.

features of these studies may affect the level of confidence that can be attached to their results. They use different measures of prices, include different factors influencing demand, and apply different estimation methods. These differences, which are discussed in detail below, may be used to discriminate among the estimates.

It is noted from the summary table, moreover, that the estimated price elasticities vary with the type of model and data used. The most obvious patterns seem to be associated with the type of data used. The long-run price elasticities derived from aggregate level data are larger in absolute value than those derived from disaggregated level data. On the basis of the former group, one would be inclined to conclude that demand is price-elastic, while from the latter group one would conclude that demand is price-inelastic. On the other hand, the short-run price elasticities derived from disaggregated data are not smaller (in absolute value) than their aggregate counterparts; rather, they are slightly larger. Thus, one gets a different picture of the way consumption adjusts over time to a price change. The initial shock of a price change appears to be relatively more important in the estimates derived from disaggregated data, compared with estimates based on aggregate data, and the cumulative effects over time are relatively unimportant. In addition, though they are less apparent, there are differences among models of various kinds that use marginal rather than average measures of the price of electricity. Elasticity estimates related to marginal prices tend to be smaller than those related to average prices.

Looking at the price elasticities according to type of model, one may conclude that the dynamic consumption models produce the greatest disparities in the estimates. Even estimates derived within the same study, using different sample periods or model specifications, give erratic conclusions about consumption behavior. This observation will be reinforced in the discussion of individual studies below. The static models that use aggregate level data, particularly those using average prices, yield remarkably stable price elasticities. The results are similar whether they are derived from cross-section or pooled data, whether state, city, or utility district data are used, and whether the samples refer to early or recent periods. From these models one is led to conclude that residential demand is price-elastic. The structural models, in contrast, show demand to be price-inelastic, and that a larger proportion of the demand response is effected in the first year of the price change.

There are no major patterns among the income elasticities. The only consistent feature is that the fuel shares models show income to be unimportant in determining fuel choices. Otherwise, the estimates show up as statistically insignificant in some cases, and very important in others. The erratic behavior of the income elasticities leads one to suspect that income may be correlated with other variables. This may be expected, for example, in regressions that include household characteristics that are income-related, such as the number of rooms and the number of appliances.

From this brief overview, one may conclude that statistical results are affected by the type of model and data used in the analysis, and that various estimates should not be given equal weight in selecting a value for decision-making or forecasting purposes. There are, in addition, other distinguishing features among the studies that are not revealed in the summary table. The following sections examine in more detail the studies within each category of the table in order to provide a basis for evaluating their results.

Reduced-form models

The reduced-form models, it will be recalled from the discussion in chapter 2, combine the separate elements of demand in a single equation. This section examines three groups of reduced-form models: the static and dynamic consumption models that estimate electricity consumption directly, and the fuel shares models that estimate electricity consumption as a share of total residential energy demand. The discussion separates the studies according to the level of aggregation of data and the measure of electricity prices.

Static consumption models. The static consumption models customarily use time-series data to measure short-run adjustments in consumption behavior and cross-section or pooled data to measure long-run adjustments. The assumptions and misgivings associated with each were discussed in chapter 2. There are perceptible differences in the performance of the static models, depending on whether time-series or cross-section data are used separately or pooled together. The differences seem to affect the performance of income and other variables more than the price of electricity. Fisher and Kaysen (1962) include only the average price and income variables in their time series regressions for each state and obtain erratic and frequently insignificant coefficients. When the states are grouped by similar characteristics, in this case by the degree of urbanization, the coefficients become significant and comparable.

Moore (1970), Wilson (1971), and Anderson (1973) use only cross-section data to fit their static models, and obtain similarly poor results. Moore estimates average sales to residential customers across 407 utility companies in 1963 on the basis of the average price of electricity, the average price of gas, and regional dummy variables to reflect climatic and geographic differences (income was not included because of lack of data). The dummy variables are not significant and the price of gas appears more important than the price of electricity. Wilson estimates average consumption per household across seventy-seven large U.S. cities in 1966, adding measures of income, average number of rooms per household, and number of degree-days, but only the coefficients of average price of electricity and natural gas are significantly different from zero. Anderson compares estimates of average consumption per customer across states in 1960 and in 1970 to examine parameter stability. The coefficient of the price of electricity remains stable, but that of income does not (see table 3-1), while the coefficients of prices of other fuels, and of climatic and demographic variables, are either insignificant or have the wrong sign in one or both periods.

In contrast, Charles River Associates (1976) reestimated Anderson's model with pooled time series of state observations during 1966–72 and obtained significant coefficients for all variables. The price coefficient, however, closely approximates the magnitude of the cross-section models. Similarly, Halvorsen (1978) used pooled state data for 1961–69 to estimate his static equations and achieved highly significant results. Again, the price coefficient is near that of the other static models.

Evidently there is insufficient variation in income and other variables, over time or across geographic units, to generate separate estimates of income and price elasticities. This may be explained in part by the process of deflating and averaging income over households or population in broad geographic aggregates, which tends to reduce variation. The problem of insufficient variation in explanatory variables is, moreover, exacerbated in log-linear equation forms. As noted by Deaton (1974), models of this kind enforce an approximate linear relationship between income and price elasticities that tends to allow independent measurement of only one elasticity.

The magnitudes of the estimated price elasticities are also remarkably stable across various measures of average prices. Moore, Wilson, and Anderson use "typical electric bills" (TEBs) at different levels of consumption (250, 500, and 1,000 kWh per month, respectively) while Halvorsen uses a measure of average sales revenues. Charles River Associates experimented with the effects of different measures of average prices and found remarkable stability among the price coefficients across different TEBs and average revenues. However, the coefficient declined markedly when differences between TEBs were used. This is worth keeping in mind in connection with studies using marginal rather than average prices, as differences in TEBs is a common measure of the marginal price. In addition, while the price coefficient remained stable across different measures of the average price, the coefficients of other variables did not. Magnitudes shifted markedly, signs changed, and significance levels altered across regressions that differed only in the definition of the price variable.

All the studies just mentioned treat the price of electricity as an exogenous variable whose values do not vary systematically with the quantity of consumption. The usual assumption is that supply is perfectly elastic. In the electricity market, this assumption is frequently justified on the ground that prices are regulated by public utility commissions and do not respond to market forces. Moore tests the effectiveness of regulation by comparing various characteristics of investor-owned and publicly owned utilities. The tests focus on the excess capacity hypothesis of Averch and Johnson (1962). With each test, he finds no significant difference in the operations of the two groups of utilities, contrary to the supposed effects of regulations. He cautions, as a result, that price may not be assumed to be set exogenously by regulation and that supply factors will affect prices as consumption changes. There is, in other words, an identification problem that could bias observed price elasticities. Moore argues that price elasticities will be biased toward zero because the marginal cost of generating electricity is positively correlated with the cost of fuels competitive with electricity. Shifts in demand and supply will be positively correlated, in other words, reducing the apparent price change associated with a shift in consumption.

Halvorsen (1978) and McFadden and Puig (1975) represent the only two static demand studies that attempt to break the correlation between supply and demand. Both use an instrumental variables approach that involves estimating prices with a separate price equation and substituting estimated for actual values in the consumption equation. Halvorsen estimates average prices rather than marginal prices, but demonstrates that the difference only affects the constant term in a linear function of quantity, and that the constant term will not affect the coefficient of the logarithm of estimated prices in the consumption equation. Halvorsen's argument is correct for a log-linear price equation, but this specification assumes that the average price is a fixed proportion of the marginal price; that is, that the average price declines in constant proportion to quantity.

Halvorsen's price equation is further flawed by the need to rely on an *ad hoc* collection of proxy variables to reflect costs of generating and distributing electricity. The equation includes, for example, manufacturing wages, percent rural population, percent publicly owned generating capacity, and the ratio of industrial to residential sales. In addition, important variables are inevitably excluded. In this case there is no account of variations in capital costs across states, which are significant in view of major differences in the mix of hydro, thermal, and nuclear generating capacity. The fit with pooled state data is quite good, but the results are questionable. The coefficient of average sales volume implies, for example, that a 10 percent increase in volume will reduce the average price by 6 percent. The difficulties involved in estimating price equations, which are perhaps easier for electricity than other energy products, illustrate why most studies ignore the identification problem.

When estimated prices are substituted in Halvorsen's consumption equation, the own-price elasticity turns out to be larger (at -1.53) than those of the other static consumption models. One might conclude from this that Moore's argument is correct and that the true price elasticity is above his observed value because of a positive correlation between supply and demand shifts. This conclusion may be premature, however, in view of the results obtained by McFadden and Puig (1975). Their model is essentially the same as Halvorsen's in all respects except that the price equation is specified as a three-parameter function of TEBs at different consumption levels in order to allow the average price to vary in proportion to the marginal price. When estimated marginal prices are substituted for actual values in the consumption equation, the resulting price elasticity (-0.48) is less than a third that of Halvorsen's.

Another oversight common to most of these models is that there is no recognition of the importance of appliance stocks and prices. Averages of income, prices, and other variables assume that all households within the same aggregate unit of measurement are similar with regard to the stock of appliances they hold and their propensity to use them. Potentially serious aggregation biases may result. Yet, studies that include additive appliance stock and appliance price variables achieve little success. Halvorsen finds no observable relationship between consumption and the wholesale price index for household appliances. Wills (1977) adds saturation rates for different appliances to a standard consumption model, but the results prove highly unstable as coefficients change signs and significance levels. In short, grafting on crude measures of appliance stocks and prices is not a successful procedure to follow.

Two static consumption studies use disaggregated level data. The first, by Acton, Mitchell, and Mowill (1976) analyzes meter readbook data in Los Angeles County from July 1972 to June 1974, where each meter readbook combines 260 customers in the same area. The unit of observation is still an aggregate of different households, but at a sufficiently fine level to warrant distinction from the studies already mentioned. The price and consumption information supplied by the utility was merged with 1970 census data on appliance stocks and demographic characteristics, plus local weather data.

In addition to a richer data base, their model has two important features that distinguish it from other demand models. First, they weight the independent variables with saturation rates for eight different appliances to allow consumption responses to vary with the stock of appliances. The saturation rates for heating and air conditioning, moreover, are converted to measures of effective rates by weighting them by heating and cooling degree-days, respectively. This procedure therefore properly weights the determinants of demand by appliance stocks, in contrast to the additive approach, and permits elasticities to vary with appliance holdings and weather.

Among the explanatory variables, the authors include the marginal prices of electricity and gas, income, demographic variables, and residence characteristics. The model performs well when estimated cross-sectionally for each two-month billing period or when estimated with pooled data, and the estimates are consistent across two different appliance weighting schemes. The price elasticities show considerable seasonal variation, ranging from −0.4 to −1.0, while the income elasticities are stable around 0.4. The marginal price of gas is also consistently significant, with a cross-elasticity near 0.5.

Because of the quality of the data base, and the innovative ways of integrating appliance stocks, the results generated by this model must be regarded as superior to those of the simpler and more aggregative analysis examined above. One is constrained from favoring these elasticity estimates only by their limited geographical reference. Nevertheless, they must be given greater weight in comparisons among different studies.

The second study using micro level data, by Hewlett (1977), draws on household level data generated by a nationwide survey conducted by the Washington Center for Metropolitan Studies in 1973 and 1975.[1] The surveys collected data on fuel consumption, fuel bills, income, and a large number of demographic and residence characteristics, plus appliance holdings. The survey did not contain information about individual rate structures, so Hewlett estimated them from groups of households served by the same utility. Expenditures on electricity by each household in the group are posited as a simple linear function of quantity consumed, where the estimated slope term is taken as the marginal price and the estimated intercept is taken as the inframarginal price. The procedure assumes that all households served by the same utility fall into the same marginal block, but this is no doubt superior to a measure of average revenues.

Cross-sectional estimates of price and income elasticities are significant but small. Hewlett regards them as short-run measures, although this is a questionable interpretation in the context of his model. The major difficulty of interpreting Hewlett's results is that he includes so many extraneous variables, many of minor interest or importance, and several that are redundant, that it is remarkable that any variables show up as important. In addition, appliance stock variables are merely added on, instead of weighting response variables in a manner similar to that of Acton, Mitchell, and Mowill. In short, the model represents a poor use of a rich data set. Hewlett also estimates a dynamic version of his model, discussed below, but it suffers from the same deficiencies. A more imaginative use of this same data by McFadden, Puig, and Kirshner (1977) is described in the section on structural demand models.

[1]The surveys are discussed in Newman and Day (1975).

Dynamic consumption models. The dynamic consumption models represent a convenient method for differentiating between variations in utilization rates and long-run adjustments in appliance stocks without a need for information about appliance stocks. The most common version is the lagged adjustment approach which, as described in chapter 2, reduces to an equation with a lagged dependent variable as an explanatory variable. The coefficient of the lagged variable is used to transform short-run coefficients of behavioral variables into their long-run counterparts. Less common is the Almon polynomial distributive-lag approach (also described in chapter 2) which avoids the use of lagged dependent variables. As in the last section, we will distinguish among these studies by type of data and by the definition of electricity prices.

Among the six studies that measure price on an average revenue basis (see table 3-1), three use time-series data at the national level and three use pooled time series of cross sections. Two of the first three give implausibly large elasticity estimates, and differ from the third in modeling technique. Houthakker and Taylor (1970) and Uri (1976) both use the lagged dependent variable approach, the first fitted to annual national income data for 1946–64 and the second to monthly data for 1971–75. Houthakker and Taylor derive long-run price and income elasticities of the same absolute magnitude (1.9), while Uri derives a short-run price elasticity of −0.35 and a short-run income elasticity of 2.0. In contrast, Griffin (1974) uses the Almon polynomial lag method to separate short-run and long-run responses, and uses estimated prices in place of actual values in the consumption equation to reduce simultaneity between price and quantity. It is notable that Griffin's long-run price elasticity is substantially less than unity (at −0.52), and the long-run income elasticity (at 0.88) is less than half the other two time-series models. Again, on the basis of quality rather than consensus, we are inclined to favor the less elastic results.

The remaining three models using pooled data include lagged dependent variables, but differ in other details. The remarkable feature of these models is the unstable character of the elasticity estimates. Using pooled state data, Cohn, Hirst, and Jackson (1977) obtain identical price coefficients for different sample periods (−0.14 for both 1961–68 and 1969–74), but substantially different long-run coefficients (−1.16 and −0.48 for the two periods, respectively). The difference is accounted for by a shift in the magnitude of the coefficient of lagged consumption used to transform short-run parameters into long-run measures. However, the differences sometimes work the other way. Gill and Maddala (1976) fit essentially the same model to data from a cross section of 147 Tennessee Valley Authority distributors and derive short-run price coefficients of -0.49 for 1962–67 and -0.34 for 1968–72, while differences in the lagged term produce closer long-run values (-0.56 and -0.62, respectively).

Mount, Chapman, and Tyrrell (1973) add to the confusion with estimates of two specifications of their model with the same sample of pooled state observations for 1947–70. One specification is the traditional log-linear, constant elasticity version, while the other adds inverses of independent variables in linear form in order to allow elasticities to vary with the magnitude of the independent variable (recall the description in chapter 2). The constant elasticity version is estimated by ordinary least squares, while the variable elasticity version is estimated by ordinary least squares and by instrumental variables, with estimated electricity prices as the instruments. The calculated long-run price elasticity is the same in all cases (-1.2), but the short-run elasticities differ by the estimation method, not the equation specification. When estimated by ordinary least squares, the figure is -0.14 for both constant and variable elasticity versions, and -0.36 for the variable elasticity version estimated by instrumental variables.

Charles River Associates (1976) reestimated the same model using a variety of sample periods and variable specifications to test parameter stability and compare forecasting errors. The results point to the conclusion that the lagged terms, and therefore the long-run price elasticities, are highly erratic with changes in samples and specifications of independent variables. Consequently, forecasting errors tend to be quite large over longer periods of time, although short-term forecasts are reasonably accurate.

The coefficients of other explanatory variables are also unstable in these models, as are their corresponding standard errors. Unlike the static models above, the use of pooled time-series and cross-section data does not seem to help to stabilize the apparent contribution of determinants other than price. More often than not, their coefficients are insignificant or switch signs across the different regressions. Overall, therefore, little confidence may be attached to the statistical results and they should be discounted in making comparisons with the other studies.

The studies just discussed fail to take into account the estimation problems that result from the use of pooled time-series and cross-section data in a model containing lagged values of the dependent variable. As explained in chapter 2, estimators of the coefficient of the lagged dependent variable are in general biased and inconsistent, and possibly the coefficients of other variables are also affected. Consistency may be achieved with alternative estimation methods, such as the variance components technique suggested by Nerlove (1971). However, a comparison with two similar lagged dependent variable models using the variance components technique indicates that this difference alone does not account for the unstable character of the results.

The two studies just referred to are distinguished also by the measurement of electricity prices on a marginal basis. Houthakker, Verleger, and Sheehan (1974) use the simplest approach, calculating marginal prices from differences in typical electric bills. They find, however, that price elasticities are quite sensitive to the TEBs chosen (see table 3-1), while the income elasticities are less so. Taylor, Blattenberger, and Verleger (1977) use a more complicated method of calculating marginal prices, and include in addition a measure of the fixed charge in the rate schedule. Marginal prices are estimated for each state and time period from the block rates corresponding to average consumption per customer served by utilities located in the state. The statewide measure is a weighted average of the individual block rates. The fixed charge is calculated from the difference between total residential electricity sales revenues and the amount that would result if the marginal block rates applied to all sales. The log-linear specification of their flow adjustment model gives reasonable long-run price and income elasticities (-0.82 and 1.08, respectively), but a linear specification does not (-6.21 and 8.56, respectively).

The final study included in this section, by Hewlett (1977), is distinguished by the fact that it is the only available example of a dynamic consumption model estimated with micro level data. Hewlett simply grafts on to his static model, discussed earlier, the lagged value of electricity consumption as an explanatory variable. This is achieved by measuring all other variables in the equation from the results of the 1975 household survey, and the measures of lagged consumption from the 1973 survey. As in his static version, Hewlett is not very discriminating in his choice of explanatory variables, nor imaginative in the way he uses important information. What may be regarded as the short-run price elasticity turns out to be consistent with the static results, but most other variables in the model, including income, become statistically insignificant in the dynamic model. As a consequence, Hewlett discounts the value of the dynamic results and does not bother calculating the implied long-run price elasticity (-0.45).

Conclusions from the reduced-form models.   Contrary to the results reported by a majority of studies included here, one is inclined to conclude that residential electricity demand is price-inelastic. This conclusion is based on the results of studies using disaggregated level data or marginal prices. It is hard to say how inelastic demand might be, and even a choice of numbers in the range of -0.5 to -1.0 can be very important in long-term forecasts. This leaves one, therefore, without the key piece of information these studies are expected to provide. There are indications that the price elasticity varies with appliance holdings, as expected, but most studies ignore this factor or introduce it in an inappropriate way. Again, no specific numerical conclusions may be drawn from the literature. There is relatively more agreement among the studies that the income elasticity is less than unity, but the possible range of values is even more disparate. Finally, there is no consistent information about the importance of interfuel substitution, appliance prices, climatic variables, demographic variables, or residence characteristics. In short, there is surprisingly little specific information about residential electricity consumption behavior that may be accepted with reasonable confidence.

   These studies provide more information about modeling techniques than about measures of elasticities. The dynamic versions give highly erratic estimates of the adjustment coefficient and therefore highly unreliable estimates of long-run elasticities. This shorthand approach to separating short-run from long-run adjustments appears unsuccessful. The static versions are more stable overall, but caution is required in the specification of the model and the type of data used. There is evidence of serious aggregation bias and of simultaneity between price and quantity. As expected, aggregate data yield price elasticities that are larger in absolute value than those derived from micro level data. Simultaneous equation bias is expected to have a similar effect, but there is no consistency in the information from different studies that specify endogenous prices. Also, the choice of measures of electricity prices is important in connection with both price elasticities and other determinants of consumption responses. There are several alternative definitions of both average and marginal prices and, while the choice makes a difference, there is no analytical basis in the literature for distinguishing among them. In applying any of the elasticities reported here, one must be careful to specify precisely what kind of a price change is involved.

Finally, the consumption models seem to perform best with pooled data, judged on the basis of standard errors, but this standard of performance may be deceiving. Cross-sectional biases are introduced and the interpretation of parameters becomes clouded as a result. Though there is little evidence on which to base a strong conclusion, estimates derived from cross-sectional data tend to be smaller than those obtained from a time series of cross sections.

Fuel shares models.   Three separate fuel shares models are available for comparison: Baughman and Joskow (1975), Chern (1976), and DOE (1978).[2] All three use the same basic approach, but differ in details. The common procedure involves a two-step model where total energy consumption by sector is estimated first and then used in the determination of fuel shares, defined as ratios of individual fuels consumed to total energy consumption by the sector. The intention is to focus on interfuel substitution by emphasizing the dependence of fuel shares on relative fuel prices.

The procedure falls short of the intended goal by failing to recognize the interdependence of prices and quantity. The shortcoming arises in the logic of the estimating equations and in the process of aggregation across fuels. The estimating equations assume that fuel prices are determined independently of both total energy consumption and the distribution of consumption by fuels. The sequential estimation procedure also assumes that total energy consumption is determined independently of fuel shares. Thus, all fuel supplies must be perfectly elastic and price elasticities are meaningful only if total energy demand remains fixed in response to a change in relative prices.

Aggregate energy quantities and prices are weighted averages of individual fuels expressed in common heat units, an acceptable procedure only if all fuels are substitutable in different applications. In

---

[2]The DOE model is an update of the FEA (1974) and FEA (1976) models.

addition, the weights are fixed coefficients that are unaffected by relative prices. The aggregation procedure is therefore inconsistent with the basic premise of the model that fuel shares shift in response to relative fuel prices. The problem of interpreting results is aggravated in the DOE model, which uses a regional weighting scheme. The slope coefficients in the DOE equations are constrained to equality across states, like the other two models, but states are grouped into ten regions to calculate regional price elasticities by weighting the behavioral coefficients by regional budget shares. The resulting elasticities vary substantially, but only because of differences in weights, and the weights are in turn subject to controversy.

The Baughman–Joskow and DOE models suffer from the fact that the fuel shares need not sum to unity, a shortcoming that arises from the measurement of fuel shares in logarithms. Chern measures fuel shares in linear units in order to permit the necessary restrictions. In further contrast to the other two studies, Chern's equations are static forms, which use lagged dependent variables to differentiate short-run from long-run adjustments. This enables Chern to apply ordinary least squares with pooled state and time-series data, while the other two require the less convenient error components procedure suggested by Nerlove (1971) to achieve consistency. Baughman and Joskow are unable to use this procedure because of the relatively short sample period (1969–72); they use instead an instrumental variables approach, where the lagged dependent variable is estimated from the other exogenous variables in the system and substituted for actual values in the consumption equations. The sample periods also differ among all three studies, as noted in the summary table.

The three models reveal a number of similarities in the statistical results. All three suggest that electricity demand is highly price-responsive, with a long-run elasticity at or above unity. In addition, energy prices are important in determining both total energy consumption and the fuel choice, while income is more important in determining total energy demand than the fuel choice. Finally, the models are unique among those at the aggregate level in revealing important cross-price relationships among electricity, natural gas, and fuel oil. Climate variables are also included in the equations, but with mixed results.

The differences among the three studies, particularly in terms of the data used, are not sharp enough to judge the reliability of their results.

Nor do the studies test the stability of their parameters with different specifications and sample periods. While the magnitudes of the price elasticities are in rough agreement with the aggregative consumption models discussed above, the level of aggregation is a principal source of concern about the results.

To illustrate this concern, we refer to studies of fuel shares by specific end uses. Erickson, Spann, and Ciliano (1973), for example, estimate the shares of electricity, natural gas, and fuel oil used for space heating in new homes. On the basis of pooled state data (for 1965–69), they find that the share equations for electricity do not depend on relative prices. Anderson (1974) estimates fuel share equations for eight separate appliances, again with pooled state data (for 1960 and 1970), and finds that the electricity shares show no observable price responsiveness in four cases: space heating, cooking, air conditioning and clothes washing. The first two are particularly surprising because of the availability of gas substitutes. Two of the other four share equations showing a consistent price effect (food freezing and dishwashing) have no close substitutes, while two (water heating and clothes drying) have close gas substitutes. The results do not constitute a reasonable explanation of behavior and may reflect spurious correlations in aggregate data.

In contrast to both of these studies, Chern and Lin (1976) find significant price effects in the share of owner-occupied housing units using gas, electricity, or fuel oil for space heating. Using 1970 census data for the share of housing units using each fuel for space heating by state, the authors include as explanatory variables statewide aggregates for fuel prices, income, heating degree-days, and an index of the price of oil furnaces. The price of electricity, moreover, is measured on a marginal basis as the difference between TEBs at 750 kWh and 1,000 kWh consumption per month. The pattern of the results is in agreement with the three aggregate fuel share equations discussed at the beginning of this section: fuel prices are important in the fuel share equations, while income is not statistically significant (nor are oil furnace prices and heating degree-days). However, the magnitudes of the elasticities are very large, with -3.85 as the estimate of the own-price of electricity and 0.85 and 1.78 as the cross-price elasticities for natural gas and fuel oil, respectively.

To summarize, this group of studies tends to confirm expectations based on demand theory that relative fuel prices, not income, affect fuel choices, while both determine the level of total energy consumption. The question remains open as to the strength of these relationships, however.

Structural demand models

Relatively few studies have attempted to estimate the influence of energy prices on appliance stocks, as aggregate level data are poor and micro level data are scarce. Three of the four studies included here use state level data: Fisher and Kaysen (1962), Anderson (1974), and Taylor, Blattenberger, and Verleger (1977). The fourth, by McFadden, Puig, and Kirshner (1977), uses household data collected by the Washington Center for Metropoliᵗan Studies, referred to above in connection with Hewlett's analysis.

The three aggregate level studies have been described briefly in chapter 2, and, as they met with relatively little success, require little additional discussion here. The analysis by Fisher and Kaysen typifies the data problem, as the authors attempt to construct aggregate indexes of appliance stocks by state in order to estimate the ratio of the current to last period's stocks. No observable price effects are revealed by the data.

Anderson estimates fuel shares for new purchases of eight different types of appliances but, as noted above, only four appliances show consistently significant price effects. Anderson nevertheless calculates weighted averages of the price responses for all appliances to obtain saturation elasticities by fuel. For electricity, the own-price saturation elasticity is -0.8 and cross-price elasticities are 0.8 for natural gas, 0.10 for fuel oil, 0.05 for bottled gas, and 0.02 for coal. Fuel consumption elasticities are then obtained by adding to the saturation elasticities the effect of price on appliance utilization rates.[3] However, Anderson does not have an independent measure of the utilization rate elasticity. He thus works backward, by estimating a static consumption model to derive a long-run price elasticity of -1.1, and subtracting the saturation elasticity (-0.8) to conclude that the utilization elasticity is -0.3. The long-run elasticity is therefore only as good as the results from the static consumption model, which does not

[3]The cross-price elasticities do not need an adjustment for changes in utilization rates because other fuel prices will not affect utilization rates for existing electric appliances.

invoke much confidence, as noted above. The saturation elasticity is questionable, moreover, based as it is on appliance equations that perform poorly with respect to the price of electricity.

Taylor, Blattenberger, and Verleger estimate appliance utilization rates and appliance stocks using expanded and upgraded data provided by Verleger and Iascone (1977) on appliance saturation rates for eleven household appliances. Appliance stocks are calculated by weighting each appliance group by a "normal" rate of usage, based on an independent study by Stanford Research Institute (1972).[4] The short-run utilization rate equation estimates electricity consumption normalized with respect to the sum of all appliance stocks. The short-run marginal price elasticity comes to -0.16 in the flow adjustment version, but ranges from -0.31 to -0.66 in four static versions.

Long-run elasticities are obtained by adding to the short-run elasticities an estimate of the responsiveness of appliance stocks. Ten appliance stock equations are estimated separately, each containing the same independent variables as the utilization rate equation, plus a lagged dependent variable and a measure of appliance user costs.[5] The equations show little price responsiveness and, in general, perform rather poorly in terms of significance and expected signs. Nevertheless, the authors calculate a weighted average of the individual price elasticities (-0.30) and add it to the short-run elasticity to obtain the long-run elasticity (-0.46).

The analysis of household level data by McFadden, Puig, and Kirshner deserves special emphasis, as it successfully integrates several aspects of demand into a logical analytical framework. As in the preceding studies, short-run utilization rates are separated from long-run adjustments in appliance stocks. Short-run elasticities are derived from a conventional static reduced-form consumption equation, while long-run elasticities are derived from a conditional logit model of appliance saturation rates.

[4]The stock figures involve estimation problems since saturation rates refer to households and some households have more than one unit of each appliance. In addition, the mean capacity of stocks will vary by the unit of observation (pooled state and time-series data), possibly in correlation with price and income. The authors address the problem by using the variance-component estimation technique.

[5]User cost is defined as the sum of an interest rate and the depreciation rate of the appliance multiplied by the price of the appliance.

The short-run consumption equation (which includes the usual income, climate, and residence variables) incorporates three electricity prices to set parameters for the rate schedule: (1) a marginal price (measured by the difference in TEBs at 500 kWh and 750 kWh consumption per month); (2) the rate of decline in the rate schedule (measured by the difference in TEBs at 750 kWh and 1000 kWh, divided by the marginal price); and (3) the average price (measured by the TEB corresponding to household consumption). Estimated values of the average price are substituted for actual values in the consumption equation in order to reduce simultaneity with the error term, where the estimates are derived from a regression of observed consumption on various TEBs. Among the statistical results, the authors find that the marginal price variable is the important price measure, in terms of statistical significance and the strength of the price responsiveness. They find in addition that utilization rate elasticities rise among households equipped with electric space heating, confirming the expectation based on demand theory that price sensitivity increases with the volume of consumption and the importance of electric bills in the household budget.

The logit model of appliance saturation rates is based on the concept of discrete consumer choices. Three appliances are considered, with air conditioning saturation estimated separately for convenience, and water and space heating saturation rates estimated jointly as interdependent decisions.[6] The air conditioning equation includes the marginal price, household income, and cooling degree-days as arguments; water and space heating depend on the ratio of average electricity and natural gas prices, income, heating degree-days, and dwelling size. The regressions perform well, with plausible results, in marked contrast to other studies that combine the influences of appliance stocks, economic variables, and noneconomic variables.

The results are unique in that utilization rates and appliance demands have been successfully separated, using data at an appropriate level of aggregation. The models are internally consistent, but also agree with the strong points of other studies. The long-run own-price elasticity is below unity, as indicated by other studies using marginal prices, and price elasticities vary with appliance stocks. The direct income elasticity is low, as suggested elsewhere, but the model reveals the indirect importance of income effects operating through

---

[6]The authors indicate that all three appliances should be modeled jointly.

appliance portfolios and dwelling size. The estimated cross-price elasticity with natural gas (0.28) is consistent with the findings of the fuel shares models. Finally, the equations indicate a systematic dependence of both utilization rates and appliance ownership on climate conditions, an intuitively important relationship that seems to elude the other models. This study provides a standard of evaluation, therefore, on which to judge the results of other studies.

Conclusions on residential demand for electricity

A great deal of effort has been expended on the analysis of residential demand for electricity, but it is evident that understanding of the characteristics of consumption behavior is less than complete. There is unanimous agreement that the price of electricity is important and that price has an inverse relationship with consumption. Beyond this, there is considerable disagreement about the responsiveness of consumption behavior. For guidance about specifics, it is recommended that readers concentrate on the few studies that employ micro level data, integrate appliance stocks as part of the analysis, and measure price on a marginal basis. These preferred studies indicate that the long-term elasticity is less than unity, and that the impact of a change in price in the first year is almost as important as the accumulated effects in subsequent years. The same studies also indicate that income, appliance stocks, competing fuel prices, and climate variables are important determinants of demand and will influence price responses. Studies which fail to recognize their influence, or which give results contrary to those expected, should be regarded with suspicion.

We have observed that the definition of the price variable is extremely important in determining the magnitude of estimated price elasticities and that care should be exercised in specifying what aspect of the rate schedule is being measured. Where alternative measures do not appear to affect the estimated price elasticities, they do affect other parameters in the model. Marginal price measures appear to be preferable to average prices, and there is mixed evidence as to whether estimated average prices designed to reduce simultaneity are an acceptable alternative procedure.

Price elasticities are affected by the extent of appliance saturation, but there is little evidence on which to base a strong conclusion. The evidence also suggests that elasticities vary substantially with end use, but again there is very poor information on their relative strengths. One might also expect appliance prices to exert an important influence on fuel choices, but no study has yet found any observable relationship, nor has any study concerned itself with equipment supply conditions. There is, in addition, virtually no evidence to judge whether price elasticities are symmetric during periods of rising and falling electricity prices because the studies draw from earlier sample periods. Similarly, one cannot say whether the elasticities are affected by the rapidity or magnitude of price changes.

Estimated price elasticities also vary by the type of model and type of data employed. The evidence suggests that aggregate level data fitted to a consumption model will yield larger elasticities than disaggregated data fitted to appliance demand models. The dynamic models using lagged dependent variables give erratic results, and are therefore distinctly inferior to the other methods for long-term forecasting purposes. The static models are incapable of providing information about the manner in which consumption adjusts from one period to the next. Consequently, little can be said about the time path of consumption behavior beyond the initial period. There are cross-sectional variations in elasticities associated with climate, urbanization, and other regional differences, but variables designed to account for regional differences perform poorly across the various models and provide little basis for any specific conclusions.

Cross-price effects are important in the interfuel substitution models and studies using micro data, but the results are inconsistent among other models. The price of gas has the strongest relationship to electricity demand, as one might expect, but the nature of this relationship is clouded by supply conditions that are not reflected in the price. The lack of access to gas supplies in earlier periods because of an incomplete distribution system, and again in later periods because of limited supply capacity, is not reflected in the regulated price of gas. Households without access (at any price) are not able to switch fuels at measured price differentials. None of the studies adjusts for this problem, so there is no basis to properly judge the nature of the true cross-price elasticity with electricity.

The importance of income is confusing in this body of literature taken as a whole. However, some of the studies provide indications that help explain the confusion. The direct income effect on fuel choice appears to be relatively less important than the direct income effect on the scale of total energy consumption. In addition, indirect income effects are felt through appliance ownership and residence characteristics that are correlated with the direct income effects and reduce the possibility of separating their individual influences. Finally, there are problems in the proper measurement of income. Income should be measured in such a way as to reflect the permanent income of households, not averages of actual income per household or per capita. The averaging and deflating process across broad aggregates evidently reduces observed variation in income and makes it difficult to derive an independent estimate of the income elasticity. In any case, household expenditures would be a better indication of permanent income than of actual income, and studies that do not otherwise account for appliance stocks should weight the income variables accordingly in order to reflect differences in consumption capacity across units of observation.

We conclude that a great deal of the information contained in studies of residential electricity demand is mutually inconsistent and potentially misleading. Great care should be taken in the use of this research, either in direct applications or as a guide in directing future research and judging new results. There are also great gaps in the understanding of the characteristics of electricity demand. In most cases, closing these gaps will require up-to-date information at the household level and models that separate the individual components of demand. We return to this topic in the last chapter.

Commercial Demand for Electricity

There are relatively few studies of commercial electricity demand (see table 3-2) and relatively few differences among those that are available. All of the studies use reduced-form models, aggregative level data, and measure electricity prices on an average basis. None of the studies distinguishes among the many diverse establishments that comprise the commercial sector. They therefore address a narrow range of methodological issues and provide little basis for distinguishing among them.

The statistical estimates exhibit patterns similar to those obtained with the same class of models applied to the residential sector. Commercial demand appears to be price-elastic in the long run, while

TABLE 3-2. SUMMARY OF ESTIMATED PRICE AND INCOME ELASTICITIES OF COMMERCIAL DEMAND FOR ELECTRICITY

Research study	Sample	Price elasticity[a]		Income elasticity[a]	
		Short-run	Long-run	Short-run	Long-run
I. Reduced-Form Models					
A. Static consumption models					
Asher and Habermann (1978)	Pooled: monthly, 63 utility areas, 1971–76	−0.25	−1.20	n.s.	n.s.
Halvorsen (1978)	Cross-section: annual, states, 1969 (two price equations)		−1.16 / −0.56		1.38 / 1.15
B. Dynamic consumption models					
Mount, Chapman, Tyrrell (1973)	Pooled: annual, states, 1946–70 (3 versions)	−0.20 / −0.17 / −1.18	−1.60 / −1.36 / −1.45	0.10 / 0.11 / 0.72	0.80 / 0.86 / 0.88
Uri (1976)	Time series: monthly, U.S., 1971–75	n.s.	n.s.	n.s.	n.s.
C. Fuel shares model					
DOE (1978)	Pooled: annual, 10 regions, 1960–75	−0.30 to −0.66	−0.94 to −1.54	n.s.	n.s.
II. Structural Models: none					

[a] The estimates given are statistically significant at the 0.05 level. An entry of n.s. indicates not significant. A blank space means no estimate was attempted or reported.

TABLE 3-3. SUMMARY OF AGGREGATE PRICE AND INCOME ELASTICITIES OF INDUSTRIAL DEMAND FOR ELECTRICITY

Research study	Sample	Price elasticity[a]		Output elasticity[a]	
		Short-run	Long-run	Short-run	Long-run
Research study					
I. Static Consumption Models					
Asher, Habermann (1978)	Time series and Cross-section:	-0.20	-0.74	n.s.	n.s.
	63 utilities, 1971–75		-1.24		0.68
	Cross-section: states, 1969	-0.20	-1.79	0.08	0.73
Halvorsen (1978)	Pooled: states, 1946–70 (3 versions)	-0.22	-1.82	0.06	0.51
		-1.36	-1.74	0.51	0.65
		-0.10	-1.02	0.07	0.70
II. Dynamic Consumption Models					
Mount, Chapman, Tyrrell (1973)	Pooled: states, 1958–73	-0.12		0.87	
CRA (1976)	Time series: monthly, U.S., 1971–75		-0.51		
Uri (1976)	Time series: annual, U.S., 1951–71	-0.04			
Griffin (1974)	Pooled: annual, states, 1968–72	-0.11	-1.28		
III. Fuel Shares Models					
Baughman, Zerhoot (1975)	Pooled: annual, states, 1960–75	-0.17	-0.75		
DOE (1978)					

[a] The estimates given are statistically significant at the 0.05 level. An entry of n.s. indicates not significant. A blank space means no estimate was attempted.

the importance of income is in dispute. There is, in addition, the same instability in the estimates derived from consumption models with lagged dependent variables. Also, variables included in the models to capture the effects of climatic, demographic, and residence characteristics perform erratically from one study to the next.

The models applied to the commercial sector are precisely the same as their counterparts applied to the residential sector, with one exception. Here, consumption is measured as the total for the sector rather than average per customer because it is difficult to rationalize the concept of average consumption for such disparate groups of customers. Herein lies a major defect of these aggregate consumption models. Individual commercial establishments and classes of establishments use energy for different purposes and in different intensities, some with flexibility for fuel switching and some with none. Measures of personal income are used as surrogates for economic activity levels, but there is a weak connection between the two for some segments of the commercial sector (e.g., churches and government buildings) and a strong connection for others (e.g., shopping centers).

Because the models work with gross aggregates, there is little to be gained from using anything but the simplest models. One should expect little in the way of detailed information about consumption behavior and the elasticities should be regarded as crude approximations. One may hope that the estimates generated from these models are not serious distortions of reality, but there is no way to judge from available evidence. Related evidence is available in a study of natural gas demand in New York state that disaggregates classes of commercial establishments (the only such study available) and obtains own-price elasticities markedly smaller in absolute value than the electricity demand studies included here or similar gas demand studies.

A few details about individual studies are worth pointing out. The two sets of equations in Halvorsen's (1978) static model refer to two alternative specifications of a price equation. These two represent the only available examples of endogenous price specifications in the commercial sector. The first is a cost specification that estimates average prices from surrogates related to the delivered cost of electricity, similar to his model referred to in the residential sector. The second is a simpler specification based on TEBs at three levels of consumption. The estimated parameters in the two associated consumption equations are quite disparate, not only for the smaller price elasticity in the second specification (see table 3-2), but also for the magnitudes, signs, and significance levels of the other coefficients in the equation. What accounts for the difference is uncertain, but one plausible explanation is that the price specification based on TEBs behaves much like a marginal price specification, with results that compare with those found in the residential sector.

The three sets of estimates associated with the study by Mount, Chapman, and Tyrrell (1973) refer to one constant elasticity specification and two estimates of a variable elasticity specification (one using ordinary least squares and one using instrumental variables estimation techniques). The three versions give comparable long-run elasticities, but the instrumental variables approach yields implausible short-run figures. The latter disparity is accounted for by the difference in the coefficients of the lagged dependent variable. For comparison, the flow adjustment model used by Uri (1976) gives coefficients of price and income that do not differ significantly from zero. Finally, the DOE (1978) fuel shares model gives price elasticities that vary by region because of differences in regional weights used to aggregate price coefficients of the states in each region. Income is insignificant and set equal to zero in the model.

This meager bit of information is the extent of current knowledge about commercial demand for electricity. More statistical work obviously needs to be done in this sector to understand the nature of total electricity demand, as it accounts for approximately one-fifth of total electricity consumption. But it is unlikely that any additional information of value can be derived from further analysis of available aggregative level data. What is required first is an effort to collect data that distinguish among commercial establishments and end uses.

Industrial Demand for Electricity

It is useful to separate the studies of industrial electricity demand into two groups: those that analyze aggregate industrial consumption and those that analyze consumption by product classes. The latter group gives results that may be averaged to compare with the overall elasticities, and provides information about the components of industrial demand that bears on the consequences of aggregating over diverse industrial groups.

Aggregate industrial demand

The aggregate industrial demand studies are similar to those in the commercial sector in technique and data, and in the inconclusiveness of the results (see table 3-3). All but Uri (1976) and Griffin (1974) use state level data as the unit of observation, but only the studies by Baughman and Zerhoot (1975) and Halvorsen (1978) attempt to account for locational biases involved in cross-sectional data. The bias arises because energy-intensive industries will tend to locate in states with relatively lower energy costs, and because cross-state price differentials will tend to persist over time. The locational differences will be positively correlated with the price effect on consumption and tend to bias the price effect upward. Both studies attempt to account for this effect with separate equations for locational decisions: Halvorsen by estimating value added and Baughman and Zerhoot by estimating the proportion of national energy consumption in each state. Both equations are unsuccessful and the estimated price elasticities are among the largest available, contrary to expectations.

Griffin's study avoids the locational problem by using national data. Although he derives a significantly smaller price elasticity, the difference may be accounted for by other factors. The first, of course, is that Griffin uses time-series data only, which may reveal incomplet adjustments to price changes. Second, Griffin uses the Almo polynomial distributive-lag technique instead of lagged depend variables to distinguish short-run and long-run adjustments. Fina the model treats price as an endogenous variable estimated separ from a supply equation. The last feature alone cannot account fo lower price elasticity, as Halvorsen (1978) also estimates separately as an endogenous variable.

Activity levels are customarily introduced through a me value added, but the variable often performs poorly and is fr deleted from reported results (thus the blank spaces in this table 3-3). Perhaps little can be expected from crude outpu that represent aggregates over firms and industries w input-output relationships. Two firms in the same produ use processes that differ substantially in energy intensive differences widen across product classes (see table 3. consideration clouds the estimated values of price raises the question of whether they result from spuriot the data. Aggregates of industries with dissimilar

ments, which face different price schedules, and which experience different growth rates and technological changes, suggest that the observed price elasticities may be determined more by the industrial mix over time and across regions than by energy consumption behavior. To shed light on this question, we turn to the next group of studies that disaggregate the industrial sector into two-digit and three-digit SIC product classes.

Demand by industrial categories

Aggregating over firms within two-digit SIC product classes assumes they have similar input-output relationships, growth patterns, and technologies. While this is not the case, there is nevertheless a greater degree of similarity among firms within the same product class than across the entire manufacturing sector. Consequently, one might expect a weighted average of individual elasticities to provide a better measure for the total sector than that derived from aggregate industry data.

A comparison of results from studies by product classes again reveals wide disparities in measured elasticities. Table 3-4 gives estimated price elasticities for different product classes as reported in six separate studies for various observation periods. The first four columns of the table give individual elasticities that are larger in absolute value than those in the remaining columns. Moreover, the same four columns yield weighted averages for total manufacturing that are well above unity (in absolute value). The Fisher–Kaysen (1962) study gives a weighted average of -1.25 from state observations for 1956; a replication of the same model by CRA (1976) with 1971 observations gives a weighted average of -1.44; and a CRA replication of a model developed by Anderson (1971) gives a weighted average of -1.32. A similar exercise was not performed with Wilson's (1974) estimates, but the magnitudes of the individual elasticities are consistent with an aggregate measure in excess of unity.

In contrast to these results, the NERA (1977) estimates for 1963 and Halvorsen's (1978) estimates for 1962 and 1971 produce consistently smaller elasticities for each product class. Both studies give weighted average elasticities below unity.[7] In further contrast to the estimates in

---

[7]Not reported in table 3-4 is a NERA estimate for "all other" product classes, and Halvorsen's estimates for several other classes.

TABLE 3-4. COMPARISON OF PRICE ELASTICITY ESTIMATES BY INDUSTRIAL CATEGORIES

Two-digit SIC industry	Energy intensiveness in 1974[a]	(1) Fisher–Kaysen (1956)	(2) Fisher–Kaysen/ CRA (1971)	(3) Anderson/CRA (1971)	(4)[b] Wilson (1963)	(5)[b] NERA (1963)	(6) Halvorsen (1962)	(6) Halvorsen (1971)
Food and kindred products	3.22	-0.78 (-1.9)	-0.46 (-2.1)	-0.36 (-1.6)	-1.09	n.e.	n.e.	-0.08 (-0.5)
Textile products	5.24	-1.62 (-14.5)	-2.08 (-5.7)	-0.76 (-1.3)	-1.22	-0.63	-0.42 (-5.5)	-0.41 (-3.6)
Pulp & paper products	10.05	-0.97 (-4.7)	-2.33 (-5.5)	-2.02 (-4.3)	-1.48	-0.56	-0.46 (-2.1)	-0.20 (-0.7)
Chemicals & products	7.71	-2.60 (-5.0)	-1.90 (-6.2)	-1.95 (-6.5)	-2.23	-0.91	n.e.	-0.68 (-4.0)
Stone, clay, glass	10.67	-1.74 (-1.4)	-1.55 (-4.8)	-1.82 (-3.6)	-1.08	n.e.	-0.38 (-2.3)	-0.31 (-1.2)
Primary metal products	11.24	-1.28 (-6.1)	-2.07 (-8.1)	-1.88 (-6.5)	-1.51	-0.98	-0.94 (-10.4)	-0.83 (-6.1)
Fabricated metal products	2.33	0.55 (1.1)	-0.42 (-1.9)	-0.39 (-1.5)	n.e.	n.e.	n.e.	-1.10 (-3.1)
Machinery, excluding electric	1.48	-1.33 (-3.1)	-0.74 (-2.3)	-1.02 (-2.7)	-1.16	n.e.	-0.72 (-6.0)	-0.79 (-7.1)
Electrical machinery	1.64	-1.82 (-4.1)	-0.71 (-2.3)	-0.66 (-1.9)	-1.76	n.e.	-0.76 (-34.4)	-0.27 (-3.6)
Transportation equipment	1.84	0.69 (1.1)	-0.37 (-1.5)	-0.51 (-1.9)	-1.01	n.e.	n.e.	-0.43 (-5.3)

n.e. = not estimated. t - statistics in parentheses.
[a] Energy cost as a percent of value added. From U.S. Bureau of Census, *Annual Survey of Manufacturers*, 1974.
[b] t-statistics are not reported, but the authors report that all price coefficients listed are significant at the 1 percent level.

the first four columns, there are smaller disparities among the individual figures for the same product class and time period. Herein lies a danger of working only with weighted averages; the averages may remain stable even though the components vary widely. Some of the changes over different time periods are too large to represent a credible explanation of consumption behavior, and major differences among studies for the same time period are the result of estimation and sampling differences. Thus, while there is agreement among the majority of studies using aggregate level and product class data that demand has an elasticity in excess of unity, here, as before, it is well to look into the individual studies in further detail before conceding the majority opinion.

Fisher and Kaysen's estimating equation for electricity consumption is a simple double-log form, with the average price of electricity and value added in each product category as the only arguments. The model is constructed under the assumption of constant technology, where the primary source of price responsiveness follows from variations in the mix of inputs and outputs by electricity intensity. The hypothesis is that a rise in the price of electricity causes the relative cost of electricity-intensive goods to rise, which in turn causes a shift toward less intensive goods, either because of a change in the consumption mix if output prices rise accordingly, or because of a change in the production mix if the cost increase is absorbed and the relative profitability of electricity-intensive products declines. To test their hypothesis, Fisher and Kaysen require aggregative level data that will reflect commodity substitution related to electricity costs, but not to changes in technology or capacity utilization. They choose cross-state data at the two-digit level for 1956. Time-series data were ruled out because of the influence of technological change; two-digit product classes represented a compromise between possible aggregation errors and sufficient variation in commodity mix; and 1956 was selected because it was a year of relatively high capacity utilization rates. They do not attempt to adjust for locational biases and concede that their price elasticities will be biased upward as a result. Moreover, value added is not weighted across states for geographic variations in the electricity intensiveness of industries, so the coefficient of value added will be biased as well. Among their results, four of the ten elasticities listed in table 3-4 are insignificant at the 5 percent level. One of these occurs for an industry (stone, clay, and glass) where energy is an important component of production costs, thus raising concern about the reliability of their results.

Charles River Associates reestimated the Fisher–Kaysen model with 1971 data and obtained more significant coefficients. However, the coefficients changed substantially in magnitude from the earlier sample period, suggesting that the observable price elasticities may be affected by changes in the composition of output within each group. Along these lines, it is noted in table 3-4 that the largest price elasticities tend to have the largest t-statistics. For example, in column (1) the mean elasticity associated with the four largest t-statistics is −1.62, compared to −0.94 for the four lower t-statistics; in column (2) the corresponding mean values are −2.10 and −0.54, respectively, and in column (3) they are −1.92 and −0.54, respectively. This pattern may reflect heterogeneity in electricity intensiveness of each industry across states, due to variation in product mix or input mix, in a pattern correlated with relative electricity prices as suggested by Fisher and Kaysen. However, the correlations may also be due to locational decisions of firms that are based on regional price differentials. The price differentials may be expected to persist over time, giving an apparent correlation between price and consumption that overstates the appropriate demand elasticity.

Further to this point, it is noted in the table that the largest price elasticities, and largest t-statistics, are associated with those industries with the largest energy costs as a percent of value added. These are precisely the industries whose locational decisions will be affected most by regional energy price differentials. The individual elasticities will be subject to the greatest bias and, because of the heavier weights attached to them, weighted average elasticities for the entire sector will be most affected.

Anderson (1971) attempts to adjust for locational effects by estimating energy consumption by state adjusted for regional mix. The dependent variable is calculated as electricity consumption per dollar of value added (by state) divided by national average electricity consumption weighted by the proportion of total value added attributed to each state. Anderson applies this procedure to the primary metals industry in 1962 and finds that the price elasticity is smaller compared with unadjusted consumption per dollar of value added (−1.26 compared to −1.75), but it is nevertheless the same as that reported by Fisher and Kaysen for the same product class. CRA

(1976) reestimated Anderson's model with 1971 data for all ten product classes (see column 3 in table 3-4) and reports elasticities of similarly large magnitudes.

The estimates reported by Wilson (1974) in column (4) are derived from the Fisher–Kaysen model using Census of Manufacturers data for standard metropolitan areas. Again, the coefficients are quite large. Of interest is the additional analysis of this data by NERA (1977) and the markedly smaller elasticities reported in column (5). National Economic Research Associates modifies the model by replacing value added with a predicted output variable to account for locational effects, includes self-generated electricity in the dependent variable, and includes competing fuel prices in the estimating equation. Each adjustment reduces the estimated price elasticities, but the first adjustment accounts for the bulk of the difference with Wilson's figures, and by implication, with those of the other studies. NERA used the elasticities reported for 1963 to estimate 1971 consumption and found that the elasticities, though smaller than others, still overestimate consumption levels. Suspicion about the upward biases imparted by aggregation errors and locational effects appears to be well founded.

The estimates reported by Halvorsen in column (6) of table 3-4 for 1962 and 1971 are smaller still. These figures are obtained from a translog unit cost function as described in equations (2-26) through (2-30). One reason the estimates are smaller is that they are derived under the assumption that total energy consumption is constant. On the other hand, the unit cost model has the advantage of abstracting from the troublesome problem of measuring aggregate inputs or outputs, and concentrates instead on the importance of relative fuel prices. The weighted average price elasticity for 1971 is -0.66, or about half the figures derived from the first four columns of table 3-4. When the weighted average figure is adjusted to allow for variations in total energy inputs, calculated by equations (2-19) with the missing information taken from a study by Berndt and Wood (1975), the corresponding aggregate figure rises to -0.92. It is noted that Halvorsen does not adjust for locational biases in his data and that the estimate is probably too large as a consequence.

All of the studies referred to above use cross-sectional data in a static framework, for convenience as well as the analytical reasons given by Fisher and Kaysen. For comparison, and completeness, we refer to a study by Chang and Chern (1978) that uses a time-series model applied to three-digit product categories. With annual national data (from 1959 to 1974) they avoid the locational factor included in the cross-sectional estimates, while the finer disaggregation of product classes should reduce aggregation bias. However, their data are subject to errors associated with technological change over time and with changes in product mix. The model is distinguished from the others by the incorporation of a lagged dependent variable in a partial adjustment framework, and the estimation of the price of electricity with an explicit price equation. Unfortunately, the model does not perform well. Short-run price elasticities are frequently larger than unity (in absolute value) and usually exceed the comparable long-run figures given by Halvorsen. Coefficients of other fuel prices are not significant and occasionally the lagged consumption and value added variables are not either.

The authors try to account for the erratic behavior of the price coefficients across industries in a separate regression. They hypothesize that the coefficients will vary (1) directly with the intensity of use, measured by the ratio of electricity consumption to value added in each industry; (2) directly with the price of electricity; (3) inversely with the coefficient of value added because of nonprice effects on the utilization of electrical equipment; and (4) directly with the coefficient of lagged consumption because industries able to adjust swiftly to a price change may be expected to have a higher short-run elasticity. All four variables are significant with the expected signs, and indicate that variations in the price of electricity and in the coefficient of lagged consumption are most important in explaining variations in price elasticities. These findings are of interest to the design of demand models because they indicate the potential importance of characteristics that differ by industry.

Conclusions on industrial demand

While there is substantial agreement between the group of estimated price elasticities obtained from aggregate industry data and those derived from weighted averages of two-digit cross-sections, one has difficulty placing much confidence in the consensus estimate (around -1.3). The considerable instability in the industrial components, both across industries and over time, indicates that the overall estimates are subject to aggregation and locational biases. The time-series analysis of national observations on three-digit industries by Chang and Chern addressed both problems, but the partial adjustment model does not yield credible estimates of behavioral parameters. NERA attacks the problem of locational bias by treating value added as an endogenous variable to be estimated separately. The estimated price elasticities are substantially smaller as a result, though forecasting exercises suggest they may still be too large. Halvorsen's model avoids aggregation problems with the application of a unit cost function, and again obtains smaller price elasticities.

From this comparison one is inclined to believe that industrial electricity demand is less elastic than aggregate statistics indicate, but doubts remain about the appropriate measure. The same conclusion reached in the residential and commercial sectors is repeated again. In addition, virtually nothing is known about the relationship between activity levels and energy demand, but at the level of aggregation required by available data, the prospects for devising a suitable measure of output are bleak. Similarly, nothing is known from these studies about characteristics of existing technologies and energy demand, including relative energy intensities and fuel-switching capabilities. Technological change, moreover, is either ignored or inadequately represented by a time trend. Few studies treat energy prices and activity levels as endogenous variables, and none treat technology as an induced phenomenon. In contrast to the analysis of residential demand, there are no structural models of industrial energy demand that attempt to separate capital stock utilization from changes in capital stocks.

These shortcomings are perhaps more serious with regard to recent years, when energy prices have been increasing rapidly. The estimated price elasticities may be inappropriate for forecasting applications because the samples employed in these studies all predate rising electricity prices. However, there is no available evidence on which to base a conclusion. This is another major gap in the knowledge about demand behavior.

Additional research on industrial electricity demand is required. It would be most useful if the analysis were conducted at a finer level of aggregation, if it treated prices and outputs as endogenous variables in an interfactor substitution framework, and if technology could be incorporated in the model. Also useful would be any analysis that explicitly separates the components of short-run and long-run behavior in multiequation models.

chapter 4

Demand for Natural Gas

Attempts to estimate the demand for natural gas encounter the same methodological issues as estimates for electricity, in addition to the problem of disequilibrium markets caused by price controls. As discussed earlier, observations on price and quantity may not correspond to points on a behavioral demand curve and models predicated on unconstrained equilibrium conditions may not be appropriate for analysis of this market.

The organization of studies is also slightly different. Residential and commercial gas demand are combined because several studies estimate consumption behavior for the two sectors together. This combination is not particularly satisfactory because of different consumption motives in the two markets and because gas supply constraints in recent years have affected the commercial sector more than the residential. The few studies that separate the two sectors may be used to compare estimates with the combined sector. The industrial sector includes electricity generation as well as manufacturing activities. From the point of view of gas demand (and coal and oil), electric utilities are like any other firms using gas as an input in production. The total demand for gas includes direct use by consuming sectors and indirect use derived from the demand for electricity.

Residential and Commercial Gas Demand

There is not the variety of studies of gas demand that one finds for electricity (see table 4-1), and several of the studies will be familiar because they apply the same model to both fuel markets. All but one of the studies use reduced-form models, and the single exception does not give a complete analysis of the structural components. There are also fewer studies that make use of micro level data, although the one by Olson, Robeson, and Neri (1979) is unique among studies of the commercial sector in the use of data that distinguish among commercial businesses. Finally, only the studies employing disaggregated level data measure gas prices on a marginal basis; all others use average revenues for broad geographic units.

There are similarities between the estimated elasticities of gas demand and those of residential electricity demand reviewed in the last chapter. The most important similarity is that measured price elasticities derived from micro level data (which also use marginal prices) are substantially smaller in absolute value than those derived from aggregate level data (and use average prices). As before, there is a hint of aggregation bias and possibly a misspecification of the price variable. In addition, the models of fuel shares indicate again that income is not an important determinant in the choice of fuel. There is also wide agreement among the other studies that income is not important to gas demand.

The dynamic consumption models show a great deal of uniformity in the estimate of the price elasticity of gas, in contrast to the electricity studies; furthermore, the long-run figures are less than unity. Indeed, except for the aggregate level cross-section estimates, there is broad agreement that the price elasticity of gas demand is less than that of electricity, particularly when comparisons are made by type of model and data. This is not surprising in view of the fact that gas is used primarily for space heating, which is regarded as less of a luxury compared with many applications of electricity.

There is preliminary evidence that the combination of residential and commercial consumption will yield price elasticities that overstate the figure for the residential sector alone. This observation is based on the comparison of separate results obtained by Olson, Robeson, and Neri (1979) for residential and commercial demand. Their data are

TABLE 4-1. SUMMARY OF ESTIMATED PRICE AND INCOME ELASTICITIES OF RESIDENTIAL AND COMMERCIAL DEMAND FOR NATURAL GAS

Research study	Sample[a]	Price elasticity[b]		Income Elasticity[b]	
		Short-run	Long-run	Short-run	Long-run
I. Reduced-Form Models					
A. Static consumption models					
1. Aggregate level data (average prices)					
Cohn, Hirst, Jackson (1977)	Cross-section: states, 1955, 1965, 1970, 1974 (residential)		−2.04		2.18
			−1.54		1.59
			−2.42		1.88
			−2.23		1.77
2. Disaggregated level data (marginal prices)					
Hewlett (1977)	Cross-section: household survey, 1975 (residential)		−0.45		0.08
Olson, Robeson, Neri (1979)	Pooled: monthly, New York state customer survey 1976–77 (residential and commercial separate)	R:	−0.17		0.12
		C:	−1.04		
B. Dynamic consumption models					
1. Aggregate level data (average prices)					
Balestra (1967)	Pooled: states, 1950–62 (residential + commercial)	−0.03	−0.70	0.003	0.62
MacAvoy, Pindyck (1973)	Pooled: states, 1964–70 (residential + commercial)	n.s.	n.s.	n.s.	n.s.

Berndt, Watkins (1977)	Pooled: Ontario and British Columbia 1959–74 (residential + commercial)	−0.16	−0.69	−0.03	0.13
Taylor, Blattenberger, Verleger (1977)	Pooled: states 1956–72 (residential)	−0.24 to −0.50	−0.48 to −1.02	n.s.	n.s.
Cohn, Hirst, Jackson (1977)	Pooled: states 1960–69, 1969–74 (residential)	−0.15 −0.39	−0.81 −0.89	n.s. n.s.	n.s. n.s.
2. Disaggregated level data (marginal prices)					
Hewlett (1977)	Pooled: household survey 1973, 1975 (residential)	−0.28	−0.37	0.05	0.07
C. Fuel shares models (aggregate level data)					
1. Static versions					
Chern (1976)	Pooled: states, 1971–72 (residential + commercial)		−1.26		n.s.
2. Dynamic versions					
Baughman, Joskow (1975)	Pooled: states, 1968–72 (residential + commercial)	−0.15	−1.01	n.s.	n.s.
DOE (1978)	Pooled: states, 1960–75 (residential, commercial separate)	R: −0.34 C: −0.32	−0.95 −1.06	n.s.	n.s.
II. Structural Models					
A. Aggregate level data (average prices)					
Anderson (1974)	Cross-section: states, 1970 (residential)	−0.3	−2.0		
B. Disaggregated level data: None					

[a] Observation periods are annual except where indicated otherwise.

[b] The estimates given are statistically significant at the 0.05 level. An entry of n.s. indicates not significant. A blank space means no estimate was attempted or reported.

unusually rich in quality, though regionally specific, and indicate that commercial demand is substantially more price-elastic than residential demand. It is noted that DOE (1978) does not find an important difference between the two sectors in an analysis of aggregate data, but as will be seen below, these results do not warrant the same attention. Consequently, caution should be used in applying the combined elasticities in either market separately.

Static consumption models

There are very few static consumption models of gas demand fitted to aggregative level data, as the results are invariably poor and questionable. Balestra (1967) tries several static versions, using cross-sections of state data and pooled time series of cross-sections, and concludes that the results are so poor that they do not constitute a valid explanation of consumer behavior. Table 4–1 lists the elasticity estimates obtained by Cohn, Hirst, and Jackson (1977) from cross-state observations for different years in order to illustrate the magnitudes implied. The price and income elasticities vary from year to year, but consistently give a picture of a highly elastic demand response with respect to both variables.

In contrast, Hewlett (1977) derives sharply smaller price and income elasticities using the household survey data collected by the Washington Center for Metropolitan Studies in 1975 (and used in his electricity demand analysis). Significantly, price is represented by estimated marginal rates and fixed charges, calculated in the same fashion as electricity prices discussed in the preceding chapter. The fixed charge is not important and the marginal price elasticity, like those with electricity, is well below unity. The income elasticity is near zero, suggesting that gas demand responds to income like a necessary good.[1] Variables measuring heating degree-days and household size are also significant, but less consistent than price and income because the model suffers from indiscriminate use of redundant variables, and appliance stock variables enter in additive form rather than as weights applied to price and income. Nevertheless, in view of the rich data base, Hewlett's findings deserve special emphasis.

[1]Hewlett notes that the income elasticity may be underestimated because the survey is biased toward lower income households and because actual, rather than permanent, income is used.

Olson, Robeson, and Neri (1979) also derive low price and income elasticities for residential gas demand, again using a rich sample of micro data and a measure of the marginal price of gas. Their study, conducted on behalf of the New York Gas Group, surveys residential and commercial gas consumption in New York state from July 1976 to June 1977. Gas utilities supplied detailed information on individual customers about gas and electric consumption per billing period, complete rate structures, and daily average temperatures. This information was combined with a separate survey of sampled customers concerning household characteristics and appliance stocks and, uniquely for the commercial sector, information about commercial activity.

The residential gas demand regression is a standard double-log form, with additive dummy variables for gas appliance holdings. The coefficient of the marginal price of gas is always highly significant, but small in absolute magnitude. Moreover, the magnitude varies somewhat with the choice of variables included to reflect residence characteristics and appliance holdings. Their results indicate that the absolute magnitude of the own-price elasticity increases when appliance stock information is excluded, suggesting that the omission of this information could contribute to an upward bias. As expected, gas space heating is the most important among the appliance variables for the scale effect on consumption, and also for the shift in the price response.

The coefficient of income varies even more with the choice of independent variables. It is positive and significant only when the variables measuring residence characteristics are excluded from the estimating equation. This adds support to the observation noted in connection with electricity demand that income and income-related variables perform poorly when included together in additive form. For statistical (as well as theoretical) reasons the appliance stock and income variables should be entered in multiplicative form. According to this study, the income elasticity of demand for gas is very low, and appears to be dominated by the importance of household size and appliance stocks. These conclusions are also consistent with Hewlett's findings.

The authors divide their sample between upstate and downstate (i.e., New York metropolitan area) customers, because gas rates are lower and appliance saturation rates for gas space heating are higher in the upstate area. The resulting marginal price elasticities are substantially different: around -0.2 downstate and -0.05 upstate. This result is consistent with the expectation that the elasticity will rise with the price level, assuming all other variables are the same, and consistent with the different saturation rates in the two areas, as higher saturation rates reduce fuel substitution possibilities. The last conclusion is not to be confused with McFadden, Puig, and Kirshner's finding reported earlier that the short-run price elasticity of demand for electricity is higher in homes equipped with electric space heating than without. For that comparison, it is appropriate to conclude that consumers with higher electricity bills would be more sensitive in adjusting utilization rates to changes in electricity rates. In the present case, the two samples compare, not utilization rates of those with gas heating and those without, but long-run consumption patterns of two groups with different gas heating saturation rates. Thus, the sample bases are different, the earlier study separates short-run and long-run determinants, and the present study combines the two. It is probably stretching the comparison of studies too far to conclude that negative substitution effects dominate positive utilization effects, as might be implied by the lower long-run price elasticity of demand for gas with upstate customers.

Olson, Robeson, and Neri's separate analysis of commercial gas demand is of special interest because it represents the only known study of the commercial sector based on micro level data. The data distinguish among six types of commercial activities (food, wholesale, manufacturing, service, professional, and all other), and two measures of activity levels (number of business days per week and number of employees). This model is also unique among gas studies in that it includes measures of both marginal and average prices of gas and the marginal price of electricity.[2] The price elasticities are constrained to equality across all types of commercial businesses, since the dummy variables act only as scale variables. The same applies to a dummy variable for the presence of gas space heating.

The estimated price elasticities differ substantially from those found in the residential sector. Both marginal and average prices are significant, and the coefficients of the two variables are the same (at

---

[2]Average and marginal prices could not be included together in the residential equations because of strong collinearity between the two.

-1.03). A marginal price elasticity this large is quite unusual and suggests that commercial gas demand is substantially more price-elastic than residential gas demand. The marginal price of electricity is also statistically significant, but of little importance in the equation.

The indicators for different commercial businesses produce large variations in the scale effects on consumption. Food and manufacturing produce the largest positive scale effects, while wholesale business shows a large negative scale effect. These differences reflect the diversity in gas consumption within the commercial sector and the potential for aggregation bias by averaging over the entire sector. It is unfortunate that the study did not also test the stability of the price coefficients across subsets of the commercial sector. The two measures of activity levels, business days and number of employees, did not reveal any observable relation to gas consumption.

In concluding this section, it should be emphasized that the two studies employing survey data necessarily limit their analysis to the subset of the market that already has access to gas supplies. The survey data reveal neither the potential for switching fuel nor new demands associated with new residential and commercial structures. Rather, the data indicate variations in consumption across households that have already chosen gas service and have adjusted their fuel choice and utilization rate to past price differentials. Unlike the case for electricity, potential customers desiring to use natural gas may not be able to obtain it, either because they are not near gas distribution lines or because supply capacity is limited. Also unlike electricity, households and commercial establishments with existing gas service do not have a wide range of additional applications; electricity is required for appliances that cannot be served by gas, while all gas applications could be served by electricity. Thus, surveys of gas consumption are limited in information compared with surveys of electricity consumption. The characteristics of demand for those surveyed may not be representative of the entire market. In particular, data are expected to show more limited substitution effects than a sample that includes former customers and potential new customers. The small price elasticities obtained by these studies for the residential sector might be explained by this bias in the sample, but the large elasticity in the commercial sector does not fit with this explanation.

Although the data have limited informational content, there is a positive side. Observations on price and quantity may be assumed to fall along a theoretical demand curve, in contrast to a sample of all households and commercial establishments, as actual demand may be assumed to equal desired demand. Thus, while the surveys contain incomplete information about the characteristics of demand for natural gas, at least the analysis of that part of the market included in the surveys is appropriate. As we shall see below, none of the gas demand studies successfully copes with supply conditions in this market.

Dynamic consumption models

Balestra (1967) conducted the seminal study of residential and commercial gas demand. After discarding the static consumption framework, he concludes that what is required is a dynamic model of demand that incorporates the relationship between consumption and the stock of appliances. In the absence of appliance stock data, Balestra develops a stock adjustment model that reduces to the familiar lagged dependent variable specification. Inasmuch as Balestra's approach is the starting point for all dynamic gas consumption models, it deserves a brief description.

Balestra seeks to explain the "new" demand for gas associated with the purchase of new or replacement gas appliances. The total demand for gas G_t is assumed to be proportional to the stock of appliances

$$G_t = \lambda_t W_t \tag{4-1}$$

where λ_t is the rate of utilization in time period t. The incremental demand for gas in each period is

$$\Delta G_t = \lambda_t W_t - \lambda_{t-1} W_{t-1} \tag{4-2}$$

Part of the existing stock of appliances will be replaced with gas appliances, denoted by $R_g W_{t-1}$, and part will remain committed to the use of gas, namely $(1 - R_g) W_{t-1}$.

The "new" demand for gas G_t^* is defined as the difference between total demand and committed (or "captive") demand, or

$$G_t^* = G_t - (1 - R_g)G_{t-1}$$

$$= \lambda_t W_t - (1 - R_g)\lambda_{t-1} W_{t-1} \tag{4-3}$$

Rearranging and using (4-2) gives

$$G_t^* = \Delta G_t + R_g \lambda_{t-1} W_{t-1} \tag{4-4}$$

or, the "new" demand for gas may be expressed as the sum of incremental demand and replacement demand.

The analogous expression for total free-fuel demand F_t^* in terms of total fuel demand F_t is

$$F_t^* = F_t - (1 - R)F_{t-1} = \Delta F_t - R\lambda_{t-1}W_{t-1} \tag{4-5}$$

where R is the rate of depreciation of all appliance models and λ is the rate of utilization of all appliances (which is assumed to be the same for each appliance).

The first behavioral equation of Balestra's model asserts that the new demand for gas is a linear function of its own-price P_{gt} and free-fuel demand

$$G_t^* = \beta_0 + \beta_1 P_{gt} + \beta_2 F_t^* \tag{4-6}$$

which may be written in terms of observable gas demand using (4-3):

$$G_t = \beta_0 + \beta_1 P_{gt} + \beta_2 F_t^* + (1 - R_g)G_{t-1} \tag{4-7}$$

The second behavioral equation asserts that total fuel demand is determined by fuel prices P_t, per capita income Y_t and population N_t, approximated in linear form as

$$F_t = \alpha_0 + \alpha_1 P_t + \alpha_2 N_t + \alpha_3 Y_t \tag{4-8}$$

Equations (4-7) and (4-8) may be combined to give Balestra's reduced-form model, first by expressing (4-8) in F_t^* using (4-5)

$$F_t^* = \alpha_0 R + \alpha_1 P_t - \alpha_1 (1 - R)P_{t-1} + \alpha_2 N_t - \alpha_2(1 - R)N_{t-1} + \alpha_3 Y_t - \alpha_3 (1 - R)Y_{t-1} \tag{4-9}$$

and then substituting (4-9) into (4-6):

$$G_t = (\beta_0 + \beta_2\alpha_0 R) + \beta_1 P_{gt} + \beta_2\alpha_1 P_t - \beta_2\alpha_1(1 - R)P_{t-1} + \beta_2\alpha_2 N_t - \beta_2\alpha_2(1 - R)N_{t-1} + \beta_2\alpha_3 Y_t - \beta_2\alpha_3(1 - R)Y_{t-1} + (1 - R_g)G_{t-1} \tag{4-10}$$

This is Balestra's basic estimating equation [although he does give estimates of versions of (4-7) and (4-8) separately]. He finds that the equation does not perform well with P_t included, so it is deleted for most of his analysis. Balestra estimates a constrained form of (4-10), where $(1 - R_g)$ is set equal to unity and the lagged dependent variable is shifted to the left-hand side to estimate first differences in gas consumption; and an unconstrained form, where the estimate of $(1 - R_g)$ is 0.954 (implying a rate of depreciation of 4.6 percent per year).[3] Balestra prefers the constrained results, which give a short-run price elasticity of -0.03 and a long-run elasticity of -0.7 (compared to -0.07 and -1.44, respectively, using the unconstrained version).

His model performs much like the lagged consumption models applied to electricity demand; the coefficients are quite unstable with respect to changes in model specification, sample period, or grouping of the states by homogeneous characteristics. There are, in addition, a number of obvious shortcomings. The model ignores appliance prices, prices of close substitutes, and declining rate schedules for gas. Perhaps most important, the model assumes that the supply of gas is perfectly elastic. The sample period (1957–62) predates supply shortages, but covers a period of expanding availability. Balestra is concerned about supply effects, and tests their importance with a time variable and groupings of states by supply characteristics, but no observable pattern develops.

MacAvoy and Pindyck (1973) attempt to adjust Balestra's model for supply effects by treating price as an endogenous variable, and separating the gas market into five regional areas with similar market conditions. The results are poor, however, as only one region (Southeast) shows the price response to be significant at the 5 percent level, and only one (North Central) shows income to be significant. In fact, the price of fuel oil turns out to be more important than the price of gas. MacAvoy and Pindyck's procedure assumes that the price of gas varies systematically with supply and demand conditions, which is incorrect in this regulated market.

The study by Berndt and Watkins (1977) is of interest on this issue, since they apply a modified Balestra model to residential and

---

[3]The unconstrained estimates are obtained using the instrumental variables technique, where lagged consumption is the instrument. Balestra chooses not to apply the variance component technique that he and Nerlove developed [see Balestra and Nerlove (1966)] because of a lack of degrees of freedom.

commercial gas demand in two Canadian provinces (Ontario and British Columbia). The authors assume that supply effects will be less serious in these areas because the distribution system was well developed during the period of analysis (1959–74), supply rationing did not develop as it did in the United States, and virtually all consumers pay marginal rates associated with gas heat, where the rate schedule is essentially flat.

Berndt and Watkins estimate a double-log version of equation (4-10), which translates to a multiplicative relationship among all variables in Balestra's model except the lagged dependent variable, which is assumed to be additive in order to correspond to the logic of his model. The estimated long-run price elasticity is −0.69, or virtually the same figure obtained by Balestra from the earlier sample period in the United States. The other variables in the model perform better in terms of significance and stability if Canadian data are used, but it should be noted that a preliminary study of the entire Canadian market by Khazzoom (1977) gives extremely poor and uninformative results.

The remaining two studies listed under dynamic consumption models in table 4-1 do not advance our understanding of gas demand any further. Both use lagged dependent variable specifications, and both find the coefficient of gas price to be the only consistently significant term in their models. Taylor, Blattenberger, and Verleger (1977) attempt to distinguish among regional markets by specifying four price variables, each associated with average gas prices in states grouped according to the importance of oil or electric space heating. Contrary to expectations, however, the lowest price elasticities of demand for gas occur for the two groups of states in which fuel oil and electricity are the primary sources of space heating. Cohn, Hirst, and Jackson (1977) provide no new insights and their lagged dependent variable model, as found in other applications, gives unstable results for different samples and model specifications.

Fuel shares models

The three fuel shares models discussed in the electricity chapter have been fitted to data on gas consumption as well. A description of the models and their shortcomings was provided earlier and need not be repeated here. The results are somewhat similar for gas and electricity. In both cases the own-price elasticity is around unity or larger, and income is not significant in the fuel choice equation. The DOE (1978) model separates residential and commercial consumption, but the results do not differ between the two.

The analysis of Erickson, Spann, and Ciliano (1973) corroborates these findings, in pattern if not in magnitude. They model the percentage of new housing units equipped with gas heat, using pooled state data for the years 1965 through 1969. The ratio of the price of gas to the price of fuel oil is significant, but neither the gas-electricity price ratio nor income is significant. The stronger relationship between gas and oil is also consistent among the fuel shares models.

Structural models

Anderson (1974) provides the only available example of a gas appliance demand model. This is the same fuel shares model applied to electrical appliances, but it performs with greater consistency relative to gas appliances. Anderson estimates the share of new purchases of four appliances that use gas (space and water heating, cooling, and clothes drying) with statewide data for 1970. The price of gas is highly significant in all four equations. Appliance saturation price elasticities are calculated (at sample means) and weighted averages of the four values are used to derive the overall saturation elasticities. The own-price saturation elasticity is -1.73 and the cross-price elasticities are 0.43 for fuel oil and 0.28 for electricity.

The own-price saturation elasticity must be adjusted upward (in absolute value) to account for the price effect on utilization rates in order to obtain the gas demand elasticity. As in the case of electricity, Anderson proposes to derive the utilization elasticity indirectly by estimating a static model of gas consumption and subtracting the saturation elasticity from the estimated price elasticity. However, this procedure is even less defensible with gas because the static estimates are unreliable. Anderson concludes that, while the utilization elasticity is unknown, the long-run demand elasticity will exceed -1.7 (in absolute value) and probably approach -2.0.

Anderson's model indicates that residential gas demand is substantially more price-elastic than the others for this sector alone, and more price-elastic than the combined residential and commercial sector. If Anderson's model had performed better with respect to electricity demand, these results could be regarded with a higher degree of reliability. They also suffer from the uncertainties of supply effects, which could be magnified in a model of saturation rates compared with consumption rates.

Conclusions on residential and commercial gas demand

The studies just reviewed suggest that residential demand for natural gas is price-inelastic, and probably more inelastic than residential electricity demand. However, the information imparted by these studies is tenuous at best, as they all suffer from the uncertain effects of a disequilibrium market. In the absence of an appropriate model for this market, further analysis of gas consumption is best restricted to observations on the behavior of consuming units with current access to natural gas supplies. Aggregative level data are not suited for this restricted level of analysis; micro data at the household or firm level are required, but very few are available so far.

Even this type of data is less than satisfactory, as discussed earlier, because it does not record the full range of interfuel substitution possibilities. Estimated elasticities will likely understate the extent of price responsiveness in this market, even in a regime of price controls. This information is also of limited usefulness because the United States is currently in a period of transition to fewer restrictions on the price of natural gas. What is required for forecasting purposes is a measure of price responsiveness in a less restricted market. Analysis of past data cannot provide that information, and only a reasonable indication of the lower bound may be possible.

What is left is an uncertain explanation of past consumption behavior and even greater uncertainty about the usefulness of this information for forecasting consumption in a less restricted market. Further analysis of available data may improve understanding of past behavior but will not remove our trepidation about extrapolating it to the future.

Industrial Demand for Natural Gas

Manufacturing and electric utilities account for approximately half of natural gas consumption, yet there are relatively few studies of demand in these sectors (see table 4-2). Two fuel shares studies are compared at the aggregate manufacturing level, two static cross-section studies at the two-digit industry level, and two studies of electric utilities.

The pattern of the findings for manufacturing demand for gas is the reverse of that for electricity. The aggregate fuel shares models give own-price elasticities that are below unity and markedly smaller in absolute value than the two-digit cross-section studies. These results are surprising in view of the possibility for greater aggregation bias at the industry level. Halvorsen's model served to indicate the extent of that bias earlier in connection with electricity, but not here in connection with natural gas. The differences between the two types of models also show up in the cross-price elasticities (where they are available). The cross-price elasticities are smaller in the aggregate level analysis than in the disaggregative level analysis and, moreover, fuel oil has the weakest relationship in the former but the strongest relationship in the latter analysis. The findings, therefore, are confusing.

There are not enough different estimates of electric utility demand to create confusion. From the single estimate each of short-run and long-run demand elasticities, one would conclude that there is very little immediate response to a change in relative fuel prices, but substantial responsiveness in the longer term. This is consistent with expectations in view of the highly capital-intensive nature of the industry.

There are a number of methodological shortcomings in these studies. None of them directly addresses the problem of supply curtailments and disequilibrium prices in the market for gas. In contrast to the residential market, supply curtailments are a normal part of service contracts with industry. In further contrast, industry and utilities often purchase gas directly from the wholesale market at prices that are subject to negotiation. Thus, supply conditions, along with demand, are of crucial importance in establishing observed prices and quantities.

Studies that recognize the curtailments problem adjust to it by restricting their samples to pre-1968 observations, or by splitting their observations at 1968, the year curtailments began. This procedure is less than satisfactory for several reasons. First, the absence of supply rationing does not remove the identification problem, but eases the problem to the extent that *ex ante* demand may be assumed to equal *ex post* demand. The assumption is not completely correct before 1968, moreover, because the pipeline distribution system was not completed. In any case, estimates derived from experience before 1968 are of limited usefulness in forecasting events in later years.

None of the studies of this sector recognizes declining block-rate structures in specifying the price of natural gas. They all use a measure based on *ex post* average revenues. Consequently, there is the possibility of a specification error and no basis for inferring the extent of the error from available studies.

All of the models presented here are reduced-form consumption models. None of them incorporate the relationship between technology and energy demand. None separate capital stock utilization from changes in capital stocks. Most focus on interfuel substitution possibilities, but none treat prices as endogenously determined and none expand the range of input substitution to nonfuel inputs. In other words, there is a fairly narrow range of analytical techniques to compare.

Manufacturing demand for natural gas

The two fuel shares models of manufacturing demand were encountered before in the industrial electricity sector. The Baughman–Zerhoot (1975) model, in brief, uses a three-step approach that estimates, first, total manufacturing energy demand, second, locational decisions of firms by state and, third, market shares for each fuel. Each equation involves a lagged dependent variable as an argument and, as before, long-run price elasticities derived from different sample periods vary mainly because of the coefficient of the lagged variable. Elasticities based on the 1962–67 and 1968–72 samples may be expected to differ because of supply conditions, but the fuel share equations show a larger elasticity of substitution in the later period, contrary to what one would expect if gas shortages removed price as the decision variable. In addition, the first equation shows no systematic relationship between aggregate energy prices and aggregate energy consumption, while price varies in importance in the locational allocation equation from one sample period to another. Consequently, the final fuel demand elasticities, calculated from simulation experiments, are derived from a tenuous base.

The DOE (1978) model includes only the price of gas and lagged consumption as arguments. The equation is estimated with a time

TABLE 4-2. SUMMARY OF OWN-PRICE AND CROSS-PRICE ELASTICITIES OF DEMAND FOR NATURAL GAS IN MANUFACTURING AND ELECTRIC UTILITIES

Research study	Sample[a]	Price elasticity[b]		Cross-price elasticity[a,b,c]	
		Short-run	Long-run	Short-run	Long-run
Manufacturing					
1. Fuel shares models (aggregate data)					
Baughman, Zerhoot (1975)	Pooled: states, 1968–72	−0.07	−0.81	O: 0.01 C: 0.01 E: 0.03	0.14 0.15 0.34
DOE (1978)	Pooled: states, 1960–75	−0.21	−0.45		
2. Static (two-digit) models					
Anderson (1971)	Cross-section: states, 1962 (primary metals industries)		−1.41	n.s.	n.s.
Halvorsen (1978)[d]	Cross-section: states, 1971		−1.47	O: C: E:	0.44 0.25 0.35
Electric utilities					
Uri (1978)	Time series: monthly, U.S., 1972–76	−0.06		O: 0.05 C: 0.03	
Atkinson, Halvorsen (1976b)	Cross-section: power plants 1972		−1.43	O: C:	0.58 0.45

a Annual.

b The estimates given are statistically significant at the 0.05 level. An entry of n.s. indicates not significant. A blank space means no estimate was attempted or reported.

c The cross-price elasticities are for fuels as indicated, with O for oil, C for coal, and E for electricity.

d Halvorsen's estimates refer to a weighted average of two-digit product classes.

series of state observations from 1960 through 1975, a period in which major changes in gas supply conditions occurred. Moreover, there is no correction for locational biases. The calculated long-run price elasticity is the smallest among those compared, but the short-run elasticity is the largest. The differences cannot be explained.

Of the two static models, Anderson (1971) is concerned only with the primary metals industry. His dependent variable measures gas consumption per dollar of value added, adjusted for variations in the location of industry across states, as explained in connection with electricity demand. The estimated price elasticity is nevertheless quite large (and of the same order of magnitude as in his electricity equation). None of the other variables in the equation are significant, however, including competing fuel prices, wages, value added, or time. Overall, therefore, the gas equation performs poorly.

Halvorsen (1978) uses the translog approximation of a unit cost function that includes only fuel prices as arguments [see equation (2-28)]. Parameters needed to calculate own-price and cross-price elasticities [see equations (2-29) and (2-30)] are estimated for ten two-digit industries across states in 1958, eleven in 1962, and ten in 1971. The parameters required to calculate own-price elasticities are generally significant, but not the parameters needed to calculate cross-price elasticities. The elasticities, like those derived for electricity, are unstable over time and across industries, suggesting again that the industry mix across states and over time may be dominating the calculations.

Weighted averages of the individual elasticities are used to derive aggregate elasticities for the manufacturing sector. They are then adjusted to allow for variations in total energy demand, using equations (2-19) and (2-20). The own-price figures are -1.9 for 1958 and 1962, and -1.47 for 1971. These measures may be regarded with greater reliability than the cross-price elasticities because of the performance of individual components, but they are nevertheless subject to serious errors because of aggregation bias, simultaneous equation bias, and locational bias. Unfortunately, there is no information available on which to base an evaluation of the possible errors involved.

Fuel substitution in electric power generation

There is a large number of econometric studies of fuel demand for electric power generation, but most aggregate over all fuels as a single input.[4] Aside from the fact that one cannot derive information about individual fuel demands, there is some doubt about the validity of using energy aggregates.[5] The remaining studies provide very little information for comparison and evaluation.

Two studies do not yield reportable results. Lawrence (1972) develops a sophisticated model for fuel inputs based on a constant elasticity of substitution production function. The model assumes that the function is strongly separable in fuel inputs, contrary to intuition, and that utilities minimize costs of production, contrary to the commonly held hypothesis for this regulated industry.[6] The model is fitted to a sample of plant data aggregated over five service areas in the mid-Atlantic region, but elasticities are not calculated and the parameters do not perform well enough to make the calculations worthwhile.

Atkinson and Halvorsen (1976a) estimate fuel demand equations derived from a translog normalized restricted profit function [see equation (2-33)]. The model assumes again that utilities maximize profits. The authors fit three equations (one each for gas, oil, and coal) to aggregate monthly data from August 1972 through September 1974, but the gas equation reveals no systematic behavioral relationships, and consistently overstates consumption in forecasting experiments. The poor results are attributed to rationing of gas supplies at existing market prices.

Uri (1978) fits a unit cost function to monthly observations from each of ten regions of the country and obtains some potentially useful results. Again, the model imposes some fairly restrictive assumptions about the electricity generation industry, including cost minimization, separability in fuel prices, constant returns to scale, and neutral technical change. The estimating equation is typical for translog representations, with fuel cost shares expressed as a function of fuel prices.

Uri wishes to fit his model to observations from 1972 through 1976 and recognizes that supply curtailments are an important factor

[4]These studies include Barzel (1964), Christensen and Greene (1976), Dhrymes and Kurz (1964), Fuss (1971), Galatin (1968), Iulo (1961), Komiya (1962), Ling (1964), Lomax (1952), McFadden (1964), and Nerlove (1968).

[5]Atkinson and Halvorsen (1976b, p. 72) conclude from their tests that a consistent fuel aggregate is acceptable only for generating plants capable of substituting between coal and oil.

[6]See the seminal paper by Averch and Johnson (1962).

affecting consumption during this period. He proposes to adjust for supply effects by adding a national heating degree variable, reasoning that curtailments will occur when demand is strongest and that this occurs during the heating season in direct relation to the severity of the weather. While the reasoning may be correct, one should not expect national heating degree-days to vary systematically with curtailments since gas supply conditions vary widely across regions. Until recently, for example, the major gas-producing states were not subject to regulations regarding priority uses of interstate supplies. Other regions use little or no gas for electricity generation, or use it for peak load generation requirements during the summer cooling season.

One may separate the estimates for different regions according to their potential reliability for different fuels. The major gas-producing states, for example, are less affected by gas supply curtailments than the west central states, where gas is also a primary source of fuel during the sample period, but subject to interruption. Relatively little gas is used for generating electricity in the northeastern states, where oil is the primary fuel and coal the secondary fuel. Similarly, little gas is used in the north central states, where coal is the primary fuel and oil the secondary fuel during the sample period. Thus, one may look to the gas-producing states for some indication of short-run variations in gas demand, and to other regions for the same information about oil and coal.[7]

It is of interest that the estimated own-price elasticities for each fuel are about equal in magnitude in regions where each fuel is of prime importance in electric power generation, but vary in magnitude outside these regions. Confidence in their reliability is shaken, on the other hand, by the finding that price elasticities are sometimes more significant (statistically and in magnitude) for fuels in regions where the fuel is rarely used. In addition, one should expect a difference in the price elasticity of gas demand between gas-producing states and the west central states, where gas is also a prime source of fuel but supply conditions vary. Finally, the cross-price elasticities frequently show stronger substitution effects with secondary fuel sources in regions where the opportunities for substitution are limited or virtually

---

[7]This procedure is less acceptable for inferring long-run responses, because the long run depends more upon the availability of alternative fuels and the appropriate generating capacity.

nonexistent. There are, in other words, indications of spurious correlations.

In spite of these reservations, Uri provides a believable set of short-run price elasticities. For all fuels, in all regions, they are consistently smaller in absolute value than −0.10, a low value that seems reasonable for this capital-intensive industry where a long lead time is required for a significant change in the rank ordering of generating capacity by fuel. They are, moreover, the only short-run estimates available.

A measure of long-run price elasticities is provided by Atkinson and Halvorsen (1976b) from a cross section of power plants in 1972. The sample is restricted to plants that purchase more than one type of fuel and is subdivided into groups of plants by fuel pairs (coal or gas, coal or oil, and oil or gas). The model is a translog representation of a normalized restricted profit function [see equation (2-33)]. The estimated own-price elasticity of demand for gas is −1.43 in the coal–gas sample, but insignificant in the oil–gas sample, although the cross-price elasticities with coal and oil in the two samples, respectively, are significant and about equal (0.5). The difference in the own-price responses between the two samples is not consistent with intuition, nor with the estimated cross-elasticities.

It is difficult to interpret what these coefficients mean. Plants capable of burning more than one fuel do not necessarily reflect long-run substitution possibilities between the fuels in question, particularly between coal and natural gas. One would normally expect the coal units to represent baseload capacity and gas units in the same plant to represent peak load capacity. In this case, substitution would reflect changes in the rank order of generating units within a plant, rather than long-term changes in the mix of plant capacity. That is to say, the sample would reflect changes in the utilization of existing capacity more than decisions about new capacity. The regional distribution of plants by fuel prices and primary fuel dependence will of course be related to relative fuel prices. But the sample is restricted to plants which use more than one fuel, to the exclusion of plants that have a single fuel capability. The latter category is of equal importance in judging long-run investment decisions based on regional fuel price differentials.

The sample of plants with existing access to gas supplies has, like the household surveys, an advantage as well as a disadvantage. The

TABLE 5-1. SUMMARY OF PRICE AND INCOME ELASTICITIES OF DEMAND FOR GASOLINE

Research study	Sample	Price elasticity[a]		Income elasticity[a]	
		Short-run	Long-run	Short-run	Long-run
I. Reduced-Form Models					
A. Static versions: Aggregate level data					
Ramsey, Rasche, Allen (1975)	Time series: annual, U.S., 1947–70		−0.77		1.34
Greene (1978)	Pooled: annual, states, 1966–75	−0.19		0.24	
Adams, Graham, Griffin (1974)	Pooled: OECD countries, 1955, 1960, 1965, 1969		−0.40		0.72
B. Static versions: Disaggregated level data					
Archibald, Gillingham (1978)	Cross-section: Consumer Expenditure Survey, 1972–73		−0.60		0.40
C. Dynamic versions: Aggregate level data					
Verleger, Sheehan (1976)	Pooled: quarterly, states, 1963–72	−0.14	−0.32	0.45	1.03
Alt, Bopp, Lady (1976)	Time series: monthly, U.S., 1968–74	−0.19	−0.50	0.38	1.02
McGillivray (1976)	Time series: annual, U.S., 1951–69	−0.23	−0.77		
Philips (1972)	Time series: annual, U.S., 1929–67	−0.11	−0.68	0.58	1.54
Kouris (1978)	Pooled: annual, EEC countries, 1956–73	−0.23	−0.76	0.53	1.74
II. Structural Models					
Burright, Enns (1975)	Time series: annual, U.S., 1959–72	−0.41	−0.60		
Cato, Rodekohr, Sweeney (1976)	Time series: annual, U.S., dates unspecified	−0.24	−0.36	0.16	0.93

[a] The estimates given are significant at the 0.05 level. A blank space means no estimate was attempted or reported.

It is of interest to note in addition that the estimates are unaffected by the use of different measures of gasoline consumption or by different bases for normalizing consumption. There are two principal sources of gasoline consumption data, the American Petroleum Institute (API) and the Federal Highway Administration (FHWA). Both sources are incapable of distinguishing consumption for private or commercial use of gasoline and both are subject to variations across states with respect to the inclusion of diesel fuel, gasoline for agricultural use, aviation gasoline, or marine gasoline. Both sources provide measures of total gasoline sales by state, and adjusted series designed to approximate motor fuel sales. These various measures of gasoline sales are alternatively normalized with respect to population, the number of cars, and the number of households. Gasoline prices are taken from various sources, including primarily *Platt's Oilgram Price Service,* the Consumer Price Index, and API surveys. In view of these differences in the definition of variables, it is surprising that the estimated elasticities are as close as they are. Perhaps this agreement should be regarded as a matter of concern rather than as a source of reassurance.

Static consumption models. Ramsey, Rasche, and Allen (1975) provide the only available example among the static models that incorporates both supply and demand elements in the gasoline market.[2] Their supply equation is very simple, however, with the ratio of gasoline to crude oil supply dependent on wholesale prices of distillates. On the demand side, the price of gasoline is endogenous, and income enters in inverse form so the income effect decreases as income increases. The regression for gasoline consumption per household is fitted to annual U.S. gasoline consumption for the 1947–70 period, giving fairly large elasticities for a static time-series model (see table 5-1).

Greene (1978) works with pooled state data for 1966–75 to explain gasoline consumption per household, and adds population density, the number of licensed drivers and vehicle density as arguments. The last two variables exhibit a significant positive relationship with consumption, and the first a significant negative relationship. The price and income elasticities are small for a pooled sample, particularly when

---

[2]Alt, Bopp, and Lady (1976), discussed below, also estimate gasoline prices separately to reduce simultaneous equation bias, but do not report their price equation.

compared to the static time-series results of Ramsey, Rasche, and Allen. Greene interprets his elasticities as short-run measures, but his interpretation is debatable.

For comparison with these two static analyses of U.S. data, Adams, Graham, and Griffin (1974) estimate gasoline consumption per car across twenty OECD countries. Their sample is intended to reveal long-run equilibrium adjustments to substantial differences in gasoline prices, in contrast to the relatively stable gasoline prices in the United States over time and across states. Pooled data for four time periods between 1955 and 1969 give a price elasticity of −0.40 and an income elasticity of 0.72, while the cross-section estimate for 1969 alone gives corresponding figures of −0.92 and 0.54, respectively. The differences are quite large, and illustrate the variation between pooled estimates and cross-section estimates.

Another level of comparison is provided by Archibald and Gillingham (1978), who estimate household demand for gasoline using data drawn from the 1972–73 Consumer Expenditure Survey conducted by the Bureau of the Census.[3] This study provides the only available example of gasoline demand analysis based on micro level data. Two data sets are analyzed: an interview sample of 7,412 households located in 23 metropolitan areas, and a diary sample of 5,152 household units in the same areas that maintained a detailed record of expenditures over a two-week period. Both samples were restricted to households that did not change automobiles during the survey year and did not use a car for business purposes. The second characteristic is important because it provides a unique opportunity to focus on private gasoline consumption. The first characteristic is imposed by the authors in order that the sample reflect short-run demand behavior. The interpretation is questionable for a cross-sectional sample, where households may be assumed to be in equilibrium with respect to the stock of automobiles during the observation period.

The measure of household income used in the regressions is based on total expenditures. This measure provides a closer approximation to permanent income than the customary use of current income, which includes transitory components, and therefore represents an improvement compared with the other studies.[4] The authors test whether

---

[3]The Consumer Expenditure Survey is described in Carlson (1974).
[4]Prais and Houthakker (1955, pp. 80–81) argue this point.

coefficients derived from a simple specification including only income and the price of gasoline as arguments are affected by the incorporation of other variables. The coefficients of price and income do not change, although several of the additions are statistically significant. However, the regressions account for less than 40 percent of the variation in gasoline consumption, suggesting that the bulk of the variation is unexplained by the model.

The statistical results imply a price elasticity of demand for gasoline of −0.60 and an income elasticity of 0.40. Both are regarded here as long-run measures, contrary to the authors' interpretation. The price elasticity compares closely with other studies that do not separate private and commercial gasoline consumption, indicating that the elasticities may not be seriously affected by aggregation across different end uses. The income elasticity is, in contrast, sharply smaller than the other estimates. The more appropriate measure of income in this study adds a dimension of credibility to the smaller figure. Other results seem intuitively correct. There is a strong negative relationship between gasoline consumption and the ownership of 4- and 6-cylinder cars, and a strong positive relationship with the ownership of an 8-cylinder car or more than one car. Also, less gasoline is consumed if the head of the household is female, is older, or has a college degree.

Dynamic consumption models. Among the studies compared here, Verleger and Sheehan (1976) give the smallest measure (in absolute value) of the long-run price elasticity of demand for gasoline (see table 5-1). This study builds on earlier work with Data Resources, Inc. (1973) and Houthakker, Verleger, and Sheehan (1974). The authors use the standard flow adjustment model of aggregate consumption per capita, including in addition to lagged consumption the price of gasoline and per capita personal disposable income as predictors. They compare statistical results using two measures each of gasoline consumption reported by API and FHWA, where the unit of observation is quarterly consumption by state during 1963-72. The estimated coefficients are all highly significant and all give a picture of gasoline demand that is price-inelastic and income-superior.

Table 5-1 reports the largest of their estimated price elasticities (−0.14 in the short run and −0.32 in the long run), which are derived from the FHWA series on gasoline sales. This series subtracts estimates of diesel fuels, liquefied petroleum gases, and tractor fuels from total transportation fuels subject to state taxes. As the series provides a closer measure of gasoline consumption for highway travel, the authors suggest that the difference in price coefficients could reflect a higher price sensitivity for highway travel. In all cases, however, the regressions indicate that income is the dominant variable in gasoline demand. The strength of this conclusion is weakened by the fact that gasoline prices changed very little over the observation period relative to income, making it difficult to obtain independent estimates of price and income elasticities.

The studies by Alt, Bopp, and Lady (1976), McGillivray (1976), and Kouris (1978) use the same type of model as Verleger and Sheehan, but differ in the type of data and the specification of arguments in the equation. Alt, Bopp, and Lady use monthly observations of national time-series data (during 1968-74), add a dummy variable for the Arab oil embargo period (November 1973 to April 1974), and, most important, estimate gasoline prices in a separate equation to reduce simultaneous equation bias. The resulting price elasticities are larger (in absolute value) than Verleger and Sheehan's (see table 5-1), but the income elasticities are virtually identical. It is unusual to obtain larger price coefficients with monthly time series compared with a quarterly time series of state observations, and this could be taken as an indication of the importance of simultaneity. However, the effect of simultaneous shifts in supply and demand could go either way, depending on the direction and relative magnitudes of the shifts. The dummy variable for the embargo period is statistically significant, but unimportant in the regression.

McGillivray also uses national time-series data, in this case annually for 1951–69, while his estimating equation is distinguished by the addition of the number of new car registrations per capita and average gasoline consumption per car, and the deletion of income. The two new variables exhibit strong positive correlations with per capita gasoline consumption. The numbers of new registrations has a long-run elasticity of 0.45 and average consumption per car an elasticity of 3.12. Average consumption is simply total consumption divided by the number of registered cars, so it is only a crude reflection of automobile efficiency. Moreover, because the number of registered cars per capita is a fairly stable linear time trend, per capita gasoline consumption and average consumption per registered car may be expected to be highly correlated, but of no particular behavioral meaning. There is, in other words, the possibility of a spurious correlation.

Kouris provides a basis for comparing a dynamic consumption model fitted to European data, where there is considerably more variation in price compared with the United States during the periods investigated. In his analysis, Kouris uses pooled observations across EEC countries for 1956-73 to estimate per capita gasoline consumption. The estimated price elasticity compares closely with the majority of those discussed above, while the income elasticity is larger. The price elasticity of demand for gasoline is surprisingly stable across rather different units of observation. The higher income elasticity for the EEC sample is expected in view of the steady postwar expansion of both income and the number of vehicles.

The last study included in this section, by Phlips (1972), is of interest because it is one of few demand models that maintains an explicit correspondence between a hypothesized utility function and the estimating equation. Phlips posits a utility function that is linear in logarithms of quantities of goods, and includes the partial adjustment mechanism for moving from one state of consumer preferences and stock of durable goods to another. The first-order conditions for maximizing the utility function give demand equations for each commodity group which, like the other dynamic models, contain lagged values of dependent variables as explanatory variables. The model is fitted to eleven broad commodity groups, using national income data for 1929–67, including an aggregate of gasoline and oil. The price elasticity of demand for this composite category comes to -0.68, which is again about the same magnitude as that obtained by other studies, each using different measures of gasoline consumption, different units of observation, different time periods, or different estimating equations.

The agreement among the estimates in different contexts suggests a remarkable degree of stability in the structure of demand for gasoline, as well as similarity in the structure of demand for gasoline and other oil products. The question naturally arises in such cases whether the results reflect behavioral phenomena on the part of consumers, or whether the correlations are spurious. The latter does not seem plausible in view of the variety of data over time and cross sections, particularly as trend components, dominant variables, and relative variation in explanatory variables cannot be held responsible for the similarities.

Structural models. Two studies are available that separate short-run characteristics of automobile utilization rates from long-run characteristics of automobile demand.[5] The procedure used by Burright and Enns (1975) resembles that of the appliance demand models for electricity and natural gas. Short-run demand is estimated with a static consumption model and long-run demand is estimated from an automobile demand model. Several short-run specifications are fitted to pooled data and national time-series data, giving a variety of results. The authors seem to prefer a short-run elasticity of -0.41, which is larger in absolute value than the static estimates discussed above.

The automobile demand analysis separates the demands for new and used cars and, again, the authors experiment with a variety of specifications. Auto demand is normalized with respect to the number of households, and the price of used autos is treated as endogenous and estimated in the first stage of a two-stage procedure. The price of new cars has a negative effect on new car demand and a positive effect on used car demand, while the price of used cars exhibits the reverse relationships, as one would expect. The combined elasticity of auto ownership with respect to the price of gasoline ranges between -0.24 and -0.34 for different specifications, while that for new cars alone varies around -0.7. The income elasticity of demand for all autos is near unity, but that for new cars is about 7.0.

The long-run price elasticity of demand for gasoline is the sum of the short-run utilization elasticity and the auto demand elasticity. The estimates range between -0.5 and -0.7 for different specifications, with the midpoint of the range taken as the point estimate. In all cases the estimates indicate that more than half of the impact of a change in the price of gasoline on consumption would occur within the first year. This conclusion also agrees with the findings of similar structural analyses of residential demands for electricity and natural gas discussed earlier.

It is unfortunate that Burright and Enn's sample ends with 1972, before gasoline prices began to increase dramatically, and that the auto demand equations do not distinguish among autos by fuel-efficiency classes. We would expect the substitution in favor of fuel-efficient cars to further raise the observed price elasticity, making

[5]Several important automobile demand studies are not included here because they do not relate auto demand to the price of gasoline. These include Chow (1957), Farrell (1954), Johnson (1978), and Wykoff (1973).

the long-run response more important than that indicated by their results, and possibly changing the conclusion about the relative importance of short-run and long-run adjustments in consumption.

Unfortunately, these assertions cannot be checked, as there are very few analyses of auto demand by fuel-efficiency classes, and those that are available suffer from weak or outdated data.[6] A model of major conceptual interest that has yet to be tested against updated information is that by Cato, Rodekohr, and Sweeney (1976). Their model starts with the identity that gasoline consumption is equal to vehicle-miles traveled times average miles per gallon of the stock of autos. The short-run effect of a change in gasoline prices is reflected through miles traveled, since the model does not incorporate short-run price effects on driving habits, and the long-run price effect is reflected in the fuel efficiency of new car sales and, therefore, gradually in the stock of autos.

The equation for vehicle-miles traveled borrows from the work of Sweeney (1975), where cost per mile traveled, income per capita, and the unemployment rate are included as arguments. Cost per mile, the link with the price of gasoline, is not highly significant (a t-statistic of -1.79), and has an elasticity of demand for miles traveled of -0.36.

The auto demand model uses the market share framework for three size classes of automobiles, where each size class is defined in terms of horsepower and weight of domestic and imported models.[7] The procedure is similar to that of the fuel share models discussed earlier. First, the total demand for new cars is estimated in a lagged dependent variable specification that includes a price index for all new cars plus

---

[6]One by Chase Econometrics (1974) attempts to use SIC data that classify cars by the length of the wheelbase, but is unsuccessful. Another study by Resek and Springer (1977) estimates the demand for new cars in five size classes: luxury, standard, intermediate, compact, and subcompact. The independent variables in the five equations include the price of cars in each class, the price of gasoline, income, automobile stocks, and the dependent variable lagged one period. The equations are fitted to pooled state data for 1963-75, but the results are too weak to draw conclusions.

[7]The authors test a demand model based on commodity hierarchies, where the demand for cars of each class depends on attributes associated with each class, and the attributes may be ranked by quality level. The price of each class of autos is a hedonic price index, based on the work of Griliches (1971), where market prices are weighted by quality characteristics. However, the authors find that estimated equations do not conform to the conditions required by hierarchy theory, and revert to the market shares approach.

disposable income as arguments. Then, an equation for each of the three size classes is estimated, where the dependent variable is per capita sales by size class, and the independent variables include the price of cars in each (adjacent) size class, disposable income per capita, and the stock of cars per capita. The auto demand equations perform well, with coefficients that are statistically significant and have the expected signs.

To get from automobile demand to gasoline demand, new car shares are weighted by average miles per gallon of each size class, summed over all classes, and divided by estimated total new car demand. This gives a weighted average measure of miles per gallon for new car sales. A similar measure for the entire stock of automobiles is obtained by vintaging the existing stock of cars with exponential scrappage and usage rates, and adjusting the average mileage of the existing stock with the addition of new car sales.

Price elasticities of demand for gasoline cannot be calculated directly from the equations for vehicle-miles traveled and average mileage. Estimates are derived from simulation experiments with the equations, recalling that the short-run estimate is associated with the equation for miles traveled and the long-run estimate is obtained from the product of miles traveled and average mileage. The short-run (one-year) figure comes to -0.24 and the long-run figure is -0.36.

The short-run elasticity, like that of Burright and Enns, constitutes more than half of the total price response. Unlike Burright and Enns, the present model distinguishes among new car demands by fuel-efficiency classes and integrates this information into a consistent model of gasoline demand. It is unfortunate, however, that the sample period for this study predates the recent increases in gasoline prices, the major shifts in demand for fuel-efficient cars, and the corresponding increase in the production of domestic models that satisfy consumer preferences. As argued above, it is expected that these changes in the market will alter the observed effect of gasoline prices on average mileage of the stock of autos and increase (in absolute value) the estimated long-run price elasticity of demand for gasoline. The relatively small long-run price elasticity, and the comparative importance of short-run and long-run effects must be considered tentative. The model should be refitted with updated samples to test these conjectures.

Conclusions on gasoline demand

We have noted a remarkable degree of similarity among the various estimates of the price elasticity of demand for gasoline. All of the studies indicate that gasoline demand is price-inelastic, though not as inelastic as many skeptics may believe. The short-run estimates cluster around -0.2 and the long-run estimates around -0.7. The income elasticity is consistently found to be statistically significant, with a value near unity. Income is therefore substantially more important to the demand for gasoline than to the demands for electricity and natural gas, as indicated earlier.

A major defect in all of the studies reviewed here is that they predate the increases in the real price of gasoline and the corresponding shifts in both the supply and demand for fuel-efficient autos. For most of these studies, gasoline prices actually declined in real terms during the observation period and consumers were limited in the options for more efficient autos. The omission of both factors should generate smaller price elasticities of demand for gasoline than one would expect to exist now in view of recent developments in the markets for gasoline and automobiles. The long-run effects of these developments on the stock of autos, on driving habits, and possibly on living and working locations, could be pronounced. The cumulative price elasticity could be substantially larger than these studies suggest, and substantially more important than the short-term price effect.

These conjectures deserve to be tested with more recent data, particularly with post-1979 data. It appears that 1979 is a turning point in several important respects. The process of price decontrol started that year, so that actual prices increased rapidly and steadily. Expectations of a return to earlier conditions were removed finally and completely, and replaced with expectations of increasing gasoline prices. In addition, both automobile buyers and manufacturers have clearly shifted toward smaller and more efficient automobiles. Prices of smaller cars have been driven up and orders have backlogged, in contrast to the slack market for larger models. Manufacturers have stopped complaining about mandatory fuel efficiency standards and have begun to introduce models that will provide a fleet efficiency that exceeds the legislated minimum.

There is another problem of correctly inferring elasticities from post-1974 data. The intermittent shortages of gasoline have had an impact on the demand for autos, driving habits, and the use of transportation alternatives. These effects have driven a wedge between desired demand and actual demand, and may have permanently altered the structure of demand because of perceptions about the likelihood of future shortages. There is, in other words, an additional element in the data that should be evaluated and taken into account. Elasticities derived from earlier samples, where supplies were always available and the prospects for rationing could not be perceived, may be misleading.

Other transportation fuels

There is a dearth of information about demand for transportation fuels other than gasoline. This may be explained partly by the lack of information about these fuels and their final uses, and partly by the relative unimportance of the contribution of specific fuels and uses. Almost all of the available research in this area is connected with the forecasting efforts of the Department of Energy.

The crude estimates of price elasticities contained in the transportation submodel of the DOE (1978) model reflect the quality of information available (see table 5-2). The submodel is handled differently than are the other sectors in the DOE model. Static single-equation specifications are used in place of the dynamic market shares approach used elsewhere, and the data refer to national rather than state observations. Also, estimated equations are not reported in the DOE publication, only a description of the arguments and the long-run elasticities.

TABLE 5-2. ESTIMATES OF LONG-RUN PRICE AND INCOME ELASTICITIES OF DEMAND FOR TRANSPORTATION FUELS OTHER THAN GASOLINE

Fuel	Price elasticity	Income elasticity
Truck fuel demand	−0.545	1.740
Bus fuel demand	−0.474	0.285
Rail diesel fuel	−0.368	0.144
Airline passenger-miles[a]	−0.245	1.457

Source: DOE (1978, p. 69).

[a] Commercial jet fuel demand is equal to air passenger-miles adjusted for a load factor.

Truck fuel demand and bus fuel demand both aggregate over gasoline and diesel fuel, and both are estimated from separate equations for vehicle-miles traveled and average miles per gallon (but without vintaging the fleet). Truck-miles traveled is estimated by weighted average prices of gasoline and diesel fuel, GNP, and the industrial production index, while miles per gallon is estimated by the interest rate, the unemployment rate, the industrial production index, and the percentage of trucks using diesel fuel. Bus-miles traveled is a function of the weighted average prices of gasoline and diesel fuel and per capita income, while miles per gallon is a function of the unemployment rate and average speed. Diesel fuel demand by railroads is based on ton-miles traveled, where ton-miles is a function of the price of diesel and (curiously) railroad capital expenditures. Finally, airline passenger-miles traveled is estimated by the average aircraft operating costs (which include the price of jet fuel) and per capita income.

It is clear from these brief descriptions that each estimating equation is based on *ad hoc* collections of proxy variables, some of which are far removed from the appropriate cost and activity variables that should be represented. Without statistical results, moreover, it is not possible to comment on the quality of the regressions and the reported elasticities. In any case, the results should be regarded as highly tentative. The subject deserves further analysis.

Residential and Commercial Demand for Fuel Oil

Petroleum product sales, as noted at the beginning of this chapter, are recorded by product category only, with no indication of the final consuming sector.[8] Consequently, an analysis of fuel oil demand by individual sectors is forced to assume that certain products can be identified with certain sectors, or that the proportion of total demand associated with a sector is constant over observation units. The studies reviewed in this section combine the residential and commercial

---

[8]Data on the price of fuel oil are poor as well. Estimates of No. 2 fuel oil prices are commonly used as "the" price variable for distillates and data for different states and years are available only from small-sample surveys. As Cohn, Hirst, and Jackson (1977) report, the lack of agreement among these series is startling.

sectors, and assume that various combinations of the various grades of fuel oil may be identified with these sectors. Consequently, there is little basis for distinguishing among studies of this sector by type of data employed. All of the models included here were encountered earlier in connection with electricity or natural gas, so the discussion will be brief. Five of the seven studies in table 5-3 conclude that fuel oil demand is highly price-elastic, while one of the two remaining studies finds no observable price effect and the other concludes that it is unimportant. Similarly, the majority of studies find no significant income relationship, but two studies indicate that the relationship is strong and important. There is no apparent connection between the pattern of these results and the type of model or the measure of fuel oil used.

Cohn, Hirst, and Jackson (1977) use virtually the same model and data as Taylor, Blattenberger, and Verleger (1977), but the two differ sharply in their conclusions. The third dynamic model, by Alt, Bopp, and Lady (1976), differs from the other two by using monthly time-series data and by substituting estimated for actual prices. These changes produce a distinctly different set of results. The three fuel shares models give mutually consistent results that are similar to their findings with electricity and natural gas: demand is price-elastic, and the fuel choice does not depend on income. The reservations indicated earlier apply to both conclusions.

Anderson (1974) provides the only estimate from an appliance demand model. It gives a saturation elasticity of -1.58, but Anderson does not adjust this figure for price-induced changes in appliance utilization rates because of the absence of consumption data for the residential sector. However, a conservative estimate (-0.17) would give a total long-run figure of around -1.76, which is reported in table 5-3.

These studies also give conflicting impressions of the nature of interfuel substitution. Baughman–Joskow and Taylor–Blattenberger–Verleger indicate that interfuel substitution with oil is in general not important; Cohn–Hirst–Jackson would agree with this conclusion for electricity but not natural gas, while Chern and Anderson each find substitution with both electricity and gas to be important. Where the studies agree about what is important, they disagree about the strength of the importance. Natural gas appears to be the closest substitute for oil, which seems intuitively correct, but

TABLE 5-3. SUMMARY OF PRICE AND INCOME ELASTICITIES OF RESIDENTIAL AND COMMERCIAL DEMAND FOR FUEL OIL

Research study	Sample	Price elasticity[a]		Income elasticity[a]	
		Short-run	Long-run	Short-run	Long-run
I. Reduced-Form Models					
1. Dynamic consumption models					
Cohn, Hirst, Jackson (1977)	Pooled: annual, states, 1969–74 (Nos. 1–4 fuel oil)	−0.19	−0.51	0.50	1.33
Taylor, Blattenberger, Verleger (1977)	Pooled: annual, states, 1967–72 (all distillates and No. 2 separately)	n.s.	n.s.	n.s.	n.s.
Alt, Bopp, Lady (1976)	Time series: monthly, U.S., 1967–74 (all distillates)	−0.13	−0.27	1.26	1.70
2. Fuel shares models					
Baughman, Joskow (1975)	Pooled: annual, states, 1968–72 (all fuel oils)	−0.18	−1.12	n.s.	n.s.
Chern (1976)	Pooled: annual, states, 1971–72 (all distillates)		−1.61	n.s.	n.s.
DOE (1978)	Pooled: annual, states, 1960–75 (all distillates; residential and commercial separated)	R: −0.7 C: −0.3	−1.50 −0.70	n.s.	n.s.
II. Structural Models					
Anderson (1974)	Pooled: annual, states, 1960–70 (all distillates)		−1.76		

[a] The estimates given are statistically significant at the 0.05 level. An entry of n.s. indicates not significant. A blank space means no estimate was attempted or reported.

none of the studies takes into account supply problems for natural gas, and the fact that relative prices do not reflect actual substitution possibilities between fuel oil and natural gas. The numbers therefore provide little objective information beyond our intuition.

In summary, the estimated characteristics of residential and commercial demand for fuel oil do not inspire much confidence. The basic data are of such poor quality and the results are sufficiently inconsistent across different models to warn potential users of the danger of applying any of these estimates. Moreover, there is not enough information from different sources to help in evaluating possible measurement and specification errors. More research is clearly required in this sector, but further analysis of the same data is not likely to be useful.

Industrial Demand for Fuel Oil

Approximately 17 percent of total U.S. oil consumption in 1977 was used directly in manufacturing and another 11 percent was used by utilities for generating electricity. Demand analysis is commonly separated into these two categories.

All of the studies included in this section have been encountered before (see table 5-4). The two analyses of aggregate manufacturing data by Baughman–Zerhoot (1975) and DOE (1978) are dynamic fuel shares models. The first is applied to total sales of fuel oils, while the DOE model separates distillates and residual fuel oil. The Baughman–Zerhoot model, it will be recalled, also includes an equation for locational decisions by states, and includes prices of other fuels. The two models give widely differing conclusions about own-price elasticities in this sector, in contrast to their basic agreement for other fuels and sectors, as noted above.

Anderson (1971) and Halvorsen (1978) work with two-digit product class data fitted to static consumption models. The fuel oil consumption data are derived from the *Annual Survey of Manufacturers,* which records the volume and cost of fuel as burned, and are therefore superior to the aggregate manufacturing data, which do not distinguish sales by consuming sectors. Anderson's price elasticity refers to the primary metals industry, while Halvorsen's figures refer to a weighted average of product classes. Halvorsen's estimates for

TABLE 5-4. SUMMARY OF OWN-PRICE AND CROSS-PRICE ELASTICITIES OF DEMAND FOR FUEL OIL BY MANUFACTURING AND ELECTRIC UTILITIES

Research study	Sample	Own-price elasticity[a]		Cross-price elasticity[b]	
		Short-run	Long-run	Short-run	Long-run
I. Manufacturing Demand					
A. Aggregate level data					
Baughman, Zerhoot (1975)	Pooled: annual, states, 1968–72 (all oil)	−0.11	−1.32	G: 0.06 C: 0.01 E: 0.03	0.75 0.14 0.34
DOE (1978)	Pooled: annual, states, 1960–75 (distillates (D) and residual (R) separate)	D: −0.22 R: −0.13	−0.54 −0.73		
B. Product class data					
Anderson (1971)	Pooled: annual, states 1958, 1962 (primary metals)		−2.18	G:	1.42
Halvorsen (1978)	Cross section: annual, states, 1958, 1962, 1971 (weighted averages)	1958 1962 1971	−1.72 −0.77 −2.82	G (1971) C (1971) E (1971)	1.03 0.63 0.74
II. Electric Utilities					
Uri (1978)	Time series: monthly, ten regions, 1972–76	−0.10		C: 0.003	
Atkinson, Halvorsen (1976b)	Cross-section: annual, power plants, 1972		−1.50	G C	0.76 1.01

[a] The estimates given are statistically significant at the 0.05 level. A blank space means no estimate was attempted or reported.
[b] The cross-price elasticities are for fuels as indicated, with G for gas, C for coal, and E for electricity.

primary metals are substantially smaller in absolute value compared to Anderson's (-0.77 for 1962 and -1.72 for 1958, compared to Anderson's estimate of -2.18 using pooled data for the same two years). One expects Anderson's estimate to be smaller because he adjusts for locational factors, while Halvorsen does not, and because Halvorsen's estimates are based on unit cost functions that assume total energy consumption is fixed. However, Halvorsen's figures are quite unstable from one period (and industry) to the next and provide a weak basis for comparison.

There is relatively more agreement among the two studies on cross-price elasticities than on own-price elasticities. Both agree that the cross-elasticity with natural gas is the largest and among the three competitive fuels coal is the smallest; both suggest substantial interfuel substitution, though the figures differ markedly. The estimates are suspect, however, because gas supply conditions are not reflected in the market price, as discussed earlier, and because the price of coal does not include the increasing costs of meeting environmental regulations. The last point will be discussed in detail in the following chapter on coal demand.

There are (again) only two estimates of fuel oil demand by electric utilities, a short-run estimate from Uri (1978) and a long-run estimate from Atkinson and Halvorsen (1976b). Fuel consumption data come from the Federal Power Commission, which reports the volume and cost of fuels burned by power plants in a manner similar to that of the *Annual Survey of Manufacturers*. The short-run estimate reported in table 5-4 refers to Uri's figure derived from regressions applied to data from the northeastern states, where fuel oil is the primary fuel for electric power generation during the observation period, coal is the secondary fuel, and little natural gas is utilized.[9]

Atkinson and Halvorsen's long-run estimate is derived from a 1972 cross-section of power plants that are capable of burning more than one fuel. The sample of plants capable of burning either gas or oil yields an own-price elasticity of -1.6 and the sample of plants capable of burning either coal or oil yields an elasticity of -1.5. The two figures are quite close, although one need not expect them to be, but the cross-elasticities (see table 5-4) derived from each of the two

---

[9]Atkinson and Halvorsen (1976a) analyze monthly observations on national data using essentially the same model as Uri, but find no observable price effect in the data.

samples indicate a greater degree of substitutability with coal than with gas. The difficulty of interpreting the meaning of these estimates was discussed in the chapter on natural gas and need not be repeated here.

To summarize, the analysis of industrial demand for fuel oil, like that of residential and commercial demand, leaves much to be desired. The estimates of own-price elasticities are not consistent among studies, nor across time in the same study. Interfuel substitution is not always included in these studies, and when it is, the estimates lack credibility. The data are poor and the models are too narrow in focus. Production functions are assumed to be separable in fuel inputs, technology is neutral, supplies of fuels and associated capital equipment are assumed to be perfectly elastic, and the prices for coal and natural gas are assumed to reflect both desired and actual demands. Electric utilities, in addition, are assumed to minimize costs of production.

One is led to conclude from available research that the price elasticity of demand for fuel oil in the industrial sector is quite large, possibly around -2.0, and that interfuel substitution is strong, particularly with natural gas, but more research is required to substantiate these generalizations.

chapter 6
Demand for Coal

Coal is used primarily for generating electricity in the United States. In 1977, for example, 72 percent of domestic consumption was used to generate electricity, while 26 percent was used for process heat and boiler fuel in industry, and only 2 percent was used directly in the residential sector. Coal is also unique among U.S. fossil fuels in that a significant export market exists, accounting for approximately 10 percent of production. This sector must be incorporated in any analysis of total demand for U.S. coal. Studies of domestic demand, our sole concern, naturally focus on electric utility and industrial consumption.

Although there are various grades of steam coal used to generate electricity, depending on heat content and impurities, all of the studies reviewed here aggregate all grades into a single category. This simplification reduces the usefulness of the analysis to readers interested in regional coal demand, where the distribution of demand by grade is important. The industrial market consists of two broad categories of coal that are distinguished in some studies and aggregated in others. Over half is metallurgical grade coal that is used to make coke and the rest is classed as general-purpose coal used for process heat and as a boiler fuel.

The demand for coal is undergoing a major transition, which is in part a result of technological changes, such as the substitution of scrap steel for pig iron in steelmaking that reduces the demand for coking coal. More important, however, are the changes resulting from the implementation of air pollution regulations and, to a lesser extent, programs designed to substitute coal for fuel oil and natural gas as a boiler fuel. These transitional factors complicate the problem of estimating the characteristics of demand for coal in recent years and render obsolete estimates derived from earlier experience. This topic is discussed first before the empirical literature is reviewed.

Problems of Estimating Coal Demand

Modeling the demand for coal is straightforward in principle because coal is used almost entirely as an input in the production of other goods. For fixed technology and a given institutional environment, the demand for coal will depend on relative input prices and the volume of output. In recent years, technology has not remained fixed and the institutional environment has experienced some drastic changes. These changes imply a shift in coal demand relative to a structure of input prices and output levels. Unfortunately, the changes are such as to make it difficult to incorporate their effects in the analysis. A secondary problem involves available measures of the market price of coal.

Air pollution regulations represent the most important of the institutional changes. The regulations began in earnest with the passage of the Clean Air Act of 1967, although lags in implementation delayed their full effects for several years. As the regulations became implemented, possible plant sites were eliminated, licensing requirements became more time-consuming and capital costs for pollution control equipment were increased. In some cases industrial operations were shut down or forced to switch to alternative methods, and in other cases limitations were placed on the quality of coal that could be burned. The Clean Air Act Amendments of 1977 promised to be even more restrictive, primarily because of prevention of significant deterioration (PSD) provisions that must be satisfied before construction permits are issued.

By limiting and delaying construction of coal-fired facilities, the regulations altered the preference for coal relative to other fuels and contributed to a large disparity in the Btu price of coal and other fuels because increases in the price of coal have not kept pace with other fuel prices.[1] The disparity means that existing facilities that are not affected by the regulations have a large fuel cost advantage compared with facilities using other fuels. Even large increases in the price of coal relative to gas or oil will not reverse this cost advantage. Utilization rates will not be sensitive to price changes in this circumstance, making the short-run price elasticity of demand appear to be near zero. Existing coal-fired electricity generating plants, in particular, will tend to operate to capacity as required by final demand for electricity, not by variations in the price of coal. A reduction in the price of coal will not encourage the generation of unnecessary output, and an increase in the price of coal will not, over a wide range, alter the rank order of plants using different fuels. Short-run utilization cannot be expected to be price-sensitive, not because demand is necessarily price-insensitive, but because the cost relationships implied by relative fuel prices have been altered by regulations.

The long-run demand for coal is affected as well because the cost advantage represented by relative fuel prices is less important after the advent of pollution regulations than before. For one thing, the cost of compliance with the regulations must be added to the cost of burning coal as air pollution costs are internalized to firms. It is difficult enough to measure and incorporate the added costs, but the problem is even more complex. The regulations are themselves being changed, and they are not applied uniformly across facilities or geographical regions. There is an environment of uncertainty that contributes to an antipathy toward coal and impedes investment in new facilities. Added to this is the additional problem of substituting between coal and nuclear power. Nuclear power represents the lowest cost option for electricity generation,[2] and thus the closest substitute to coal on observable economic grounds, but the anathema toward nuclear is even more pronounced than that for coal. There are no simple measures of these ingredients and the adjustments to the changes have not reached a new equilibrium.

---

[1] In 1968, for example, the average cost of coal consumed by electric utilities was 25.6 cents per million Btus, compared to 34.1 cents for oil and 25.1 cents for gas. By 1978, the corresponding figures were 116.1 cents for coal, 222.9 cents for oil, and 141.0 cents for gas (Edison Electric Institute, *Statistical Yearbook of the Electric Utility Industry for 1968*, p. 51; *Statistical Yearbook of the Electric Utility Industry for 1978*, Washington, D.C., p. 51).

[2] See Schurr and coauthors (1979), pp. 286 ff.

Once the regulations become well defined and stabilized, their costs will become fully internalized by firms and the relationship among fuel prices, inputs, and outputs will adjust to the new reality. Just as other sources of differential capital costs and other characteristics associated with different fuels become reflected in these relationships, eventually the environmental constraints on the use of coal will be integrated. Until then, the market for coal is in disequilibrium and observations on prices and quantities are not likely to reflect desired demand. Estimated demand elasticities derived from earlier sample periods will not reflect the structural changes induced by the regulations. They become obsolete for use in forecasting exercises.

Changes in other aspects of the regulatory environment have occurred or are under way. Rate schedules for electric utilities are no longer based on invested capital alone, but include a fuel cost adjustment to account for the recent escalation in energy costs. With this addition, utilities become similar to a cost-plus type operation and there is, as a result, little incentive to switch existing capacity from higher cost oil to coal.[3] The cost differential is covered by the rate schedule, making it unnecessary for the firm to expose itself to the financial uncertainties involved in a major capital investment. Financial positions are already depressed because bond prices reflect perceptions of higher risks in this industry, and firms are reluctant to dilute equity values further by issuing additional shares. Consequently, there is substantial difficulty in raising capital, increased risk of exposing that investment because of licensing delays, and reduced incentive to make changes in capacity because of fuel cost adjustments in rate schedules. These factors all represent recent changes in the institutional environment facing utilities that will not be reflected in earlier experience; they are difficult to capture in current analyses and may alter just as dramatically in the future.

Another potentially important change in the regulatory environment concerns those programs aimed at switching from oil and gas to coal in large boilers. Mandatory limitations now exist on the use of gas or oil in new facilities, and programs are being implemented to use

---

[3]The pricing rules also distort incentives for switching among types of coal as, for example, low sulfur coal and high sulfur coal. Low sulfur coal is more expensive, but the cost may be included immediately in the fuel cost adjustment rate; while high sulfur coal requires capital expenditures for scrubbers that can be recouped only after formal rate adjustment proceedings.

subsidies to encourage or regulations to force existing facilities to switch to coal. The effect of these programs is uncertain so far, but they represent another example of the institutional changes affecting energy markets that complicate demand analysis.

These institutional factors are also important in analyzing demand for natural gas and fuel oil because there is a discrepancy between desired and actual demands at existing market prices. Restrictions on the use of coal in some applications, or inducements in favor of coal in others, will shift the demands for alternative energy sources. Similarly, natural gas price controls affect the demand for coal because price differentials do not reflect fuel substitution possibilities. And programs that affect the market for oil, such as the oil import quota program during 1959–73 and the oil price control program of more recent years, also have their own special implications for the demand for coal.[4] These programs come and go over the years, and each variation disturbs the observed relationships among the variables that are used to measure the characteristics of demand.

In addition to these institutional factors that complicate the interpretation of data, there is also a problem of measuring the market price of coal. Unlike other fuels bought by final users, nearly 80 percent of U.S. coal is sold on long-term contracts that historically average twenty to thirty years in duration. The remaining 20 percent or so is sold at what is loosely termed a spot price, which refers to any transaction other than a long-term contract. Spot prices will register short-term fluctuations in the market, but do not measure the marginal cost of coal to buyers at any given moment of time. Long-term contract prices also vary in definition, for they may record the average of new contract prices or an average of oil contract prices in force during a period, and they may be stated in current dollars or in terms of real annuities.

All of the studies reported here use a single pricing convention that refers to an *ex post* calculation of the average cost of fuel burned during the observation period. This average may therefore reflect more than one purchase negotiated at more than one time, and different firms or industries will record different prices at the same moment, depending on the distribution of purchases and contract prices averaged during the observation period.

[4]For a discussion of the oil import quota program and its effects, see Bohi and Russell (1978), especially chapter 5.

With aggregative level data, the average cost of coal burned will tend to resemble a long-term moving average of market prices. As such, the price will reflect long-term trends, and will smooth out short-term fluctuations. One cannot expect reliable estimates of short-run price responses as a result; however, long-run capacity decisions may be based more on expectations about price trends than short-term fluctuations, and a moving average is a reasonable approximation of these trends.

None of the studies reviewed here analyze the issues just raised. A few studies restrict the sample period to observations made prior to the implementation of air pollution regulations in order to avoid difficulties, but the analysis is of limited usefulness as a result. Our review is limited to econometric analyses because of the focus on price responses, although it may be argued that noneconomic factors are of dominant importance.[5] More will be said about this later.

Demand for Coal by Electric Utilities

Three studies estimate the demand for coal by electric utilities (see table 6-1).[6] Those by Uri (1978) and Atkinson and Halvorsen (1976b) were discussed earlier in the chapters on natural gas and fuel oil. Both use translog representations of input demand functions that, perhaps inappropriately, assume profit-maximizing behavior on the part of utilities. Uri uses monthly data to focus on short-run elasticities in ten regions of the United States. The figures reported in table 6-1 refer to two regions where coal is the primary fuel for electric power generation, oil is the secondary fuel, and little gas is utilized.[7] In view

[5]Because this review is limited to econometric studies of demand analysis, it ignores a number of coal models that do not explicitly base demand projections on coal prices. These models include, for example, the Bechtel Corp. RESPONS model; the ICF, Inc. National Coal Model; the Argonne National Laboratory Coal Market Model; the Charles River Associates, Potomac Electric Power Co. coal model; the Bechtel Corp. ESPM model; the Brookhaven National Laboratory TESOM model; the Gulf Oil Corp., Stanford Research Institute model; the Dartmouth FOSSIL 1 model; and the Data Resources, Inc., Zimmerman model. A review and comparison of these models may be found in Energy Modeling Forum (1978).

[6]Two additional studies, by Atkinson and Halvorsen (1976a) and Lawrence (1972), do not give reportable results (see the discussion in chapter 4).

[7]One region includes Delaware, District of Columbia, Maryland, Pennsylvania, Virginia, and West Virginia; the second region includes Illinois, Indiana, Michigan, Minnesota, Ohio, and Wisconsin.

TABLE 6-1. SUMMARY OF ESTIMATED PRICE ELASTICITIES OF DEMAND FOR COAL BY ELECTRIC UTILITIES

		Own-price elasticity[a]		Cross-price elasticity[b]	
Research study	Sample	Short-run	Long-run	Short-run	Long-run
Reddy (1974)	Time series: annual, U.S., 1956–71	−0.46	−0.67	O: 0.26 G. n.s.	0.38 n.s.
Uri (1978)	Time series: monthly, regions, 1972–76	−0.09		O: 0.02 G: n.s.	
Atkinson, Halvorsen (1976b)	Cross-section: annual, power plants, 1972		−1.15	O: G:	0.99 n.s.

a The estimates given are statistically significant at the 0.05 level. An entry of n.s. indicates not significant. A blank space means no estimate was attempted or reported.

b The cross-price elasticities are for fuels as indicated, with O for oil and G for gas.

of our earlier discussion, it is not surprising that the short-run price elasticities are very small.

For comparison, Halvorsen fits his model to cross-sections of power plants capable of burning more than one fuel. The estimates indicate considerable price sensitivity and substantial interfuel substitution between oil and coal. We question the meaning of the estimates, as discussed in chapter 4, because of the restricted nature of the sample. The sample of plants capable of burning coal and another fuel is not necessarily representative of long-term adjustments to geographical price differentials compared with a sample of all coal-burning plants. Dual fuel capability is not representative of interfuel substitution in a long-run sense.

Reddy (1974) estimates a more traditional model based on fuel prices and electricity output (which is also based on the assumption of profit maximization). Static and flow adjustment versions, each expressed in linear and log-linear forms, are fitted to annual national data for 1956–71. With the exception of the price of gas, all coefficients are significant with the expected signs. However, the magnitudes of the coefficients are not always plausible. The short-run own-price elasticity in the dynamic version (−0.46) seems implausibly large for this industry, and may be biased by the average price measure used, as suggested by the discussion in the previous section. The long-run measure is more reasonable (−0.67) and is close to the static estimate, but is derived from an adjustment coefficient (0.31) that implies an almost immediate response to price changes. Consequently, the estimates of price sensitivity are suspect.

The three models provide very little information that is mutually consistent. Only the unimportance of the price of natural gas is common to all three. There is no basis for choosing one set of estimates over another, however, as all three studies suffer from data problems and apply demand models that are questionable in the context of this industry.

Demand for Coal in Manufacturing

Five studies analyze the demand for coal in manufacturing (see table 6-2), and all but that of Reddy (1974) have been discussed already in the chapters on electricity, natural gas, and fuel oil. There is little comparability among their respective estimates because some studies distinguish between coking coal and steam coal, while others combine the two, and some studies aggregate demand for industries while others distinguish among product classes. The distinctions are of some importance, however, as the bulk of coking coal is used in the primary metals industry alone.

Reddy (1974) estimates separate equations for coking coal and steam coal, both of which use lagged consumption as explanatory variables. Coking coal is related to its price and pig iron production, while steam coal is related to its price and the index of industrial production. Steam coal appears to be much more price-elastic than coking coal (see table 6-2). DOE (1978) also estimates the two types of coal separately; coking coal with a static consumption model and steam coal with the dynamic fuel shares model (as applied in other sectors). In contrast to Reddy's estimates, coking coal demand appears to be price-insensitive and steam coal demand is price-inelastic. Baughman and Zerhoot (1975) combine both types in their fuel shares model and obtain a long-run price elasticity that could be interpreted as an average of the separate elasticities derived by Reddy.

Turning to the two studies of two-digit product classes, Anderson (1971) focuses exclusively on the primary metals industry with his static consumption model. Separate equations for coking coal and steam coal indicate that the first is price-elastic and the second is

TABLE 6-2. SUMMARY OF ESTIMATED PRICE ELASTICITIES OF DEMAND FOR COAL IN MANUFACTURING

Research study	Sample	Own-price elasticity[a]		Cross-price elasticity[b]	
		Short-run	Long-run	Short-run	Long-run
I. Aggregate Level Data					
Reddy (1974)	Time series: annual, U.S., 1956–71				
	Coking coal	−0.25	−0.55		
	Steam coal	−0.49	−2.06		
Baughman, Zerhoot	Pooled: annual, states, 1968–72 (all coal)	−0.10	−1.14	O: 0.01	0.14
				G: 0.06	0.75
				E: 0.03	0.33
DOE (1978)	Coking coal: time series: annual, U.S., 1960–75		n.s.		
	Steam coal: pooled states, 1960–75	−0.28	−0.49		
II. Product Class Data					
Anderson (1971)	Pooled: annual, states, 1958, 1962 (primary metals)				
	Coking coal		−1.14	O	3.06
				E	−1.35
	Steam coal		n.s.	O	1.66
				G	1.03
Halvorsen (1978)	Cross-section: annual, states, 1971 (all coal)				
	Stone, glass, clay		−2.22	O	0.83
				G	1.27
	Primary metals		−1.53	O	1.92
				E	n.s.
	Fabricated metal products		−2.00	O	n.s.
				G	n.s.

[a] The estimates given are statistically significant at the 0.05 level. An entry of n.s. indicates not significant. A blank space means no estimate was attempted or reported.
[b] The cross-price elasticities are for fuels as indicated, with O for oil, G for gas, and E for electricity.

completely unresponsive to its price. These findings do not agree with those of Reddy and DOE, which suggest that coking coal is less responsive to price than steam coal, or not price responsive at all. Anderson's results are somewhat more credible with respect to coking coal because primary metals is the major consuming industry. However, the regression gives an implausibly large cross-price elasticity with oil (3.06) and a negative cross-price elasticity with electricity (-1.35). The last result probably reflects the technological shift to scrap steel processes that use electric arc furnaces. The steam coal equation suggests that consumption is closely related to oil and gas prices, but not its own-price, and thus runs contrary to theoretical expectations.

Halvorsen (1978) estimates coal demand in several two-digit industries. Table 6-2 reports the price elasticities for three product classes for which the regressions perform well and, not coincidentally, for which coal is an important energy source. The data do not separate coking coal and steam coal, but the results with primary metals may be identified with coking coal and the others with steam coal. The figures for primary metals are comparable to those given by Anderson for coking coal, and the others are consistent with Reddy's figures for steam coal. This is about the only corroboration one can find among these studies.

Conclusion

The review of empirical studies indicates that very little is known about the characteristics of coal demand. There is substantial disagreement among the results and insufficient information to make judgments about the reasons for the discrepancies. Most of the studies use older data that, while not significantly distorted by the institutional changes discussed, are also incapable of reflecting the importance of these changes. Thus, little is known about demand behavior during earlier periods and even less about the applicability of this information for current and future periods.

The majority of long-run estimates indicate that the demand for coal is price-elastic, but this information must be heavily discounted. There has been a gradual downtrend in the use of coal over many years, and a corresponding uptrend in the price of coal, which makes a strong negative price relationship inevitable in time-series models. However, the two trends do not reflect movements along a stable demand curve, but rather the combination of shifts in supply and demand that accompany technological developments, coal mining and use regulations, and developments in other fuel markets. None of these factors have been incorporated in the analysis to help in judging the importance of price effects on demand.

chapter 7

Summary and Conclusions

The variety and severity of estimation problems discussed in the preceding chapters demonstrate that it is no simple matter to estimate price elasticities and that it is equally difficult to assess the reliability of the estimates that have been made. Comparisons of estimation procedures indicate that potentially large discrepancies may occur as a result of choices among competing models, estimators, and data. The tools of econometrics are not capable of answering many of the questions to which they are applied, and should not be expected to answer others. Nevertheless, this technique is the only one we have for obtaining certain kinds of information and, properly applied, can provide helpful insights into the results of policy decisions.

We draw a number of conclusions about existing estimation methods and empirical results that should be kept in mind by both analysts and those using their findings. Our evaluation concentrates on the reliability and defensibility of the measures available for each energy submarket and the relative efficacy of different estimation approaches. Finally, we discuss some inherent limitations of econometric analysis and their implications for those who use it.

Estimation Problems

Estimation problems revolve around five major issues: (1) capturing the dynamics of demand, (2) determining the appropriate level of

146

aggregation, (3) identifying the separate influences on demand, (4) separating supply from demand effects, and (5) using appropriate equation forms and estimation techniques.

Capturing the dynamics of demand

The demand for energy products is a dynamic process because it depends on both the rate at which the existing stock of durable equipment is used and on changes in the stock. In the empirical literature examined here, the distinction between stock utilization and stock adjustment is reduced to a dichotomization between short-run and long-run adjustments in consumption, with the length of time for each either unspecified or determined by the data. These models do not fully capture the temporal nature of energy demand.

It seems most useful to give up the notion that dynamics can be adequately reflected in any model that strictly separates single-period from infinite-period adjustments. This dichotomization is particularly meaningless when it is applied to groups of consumers because capital stock decisions are made continuously through all periods. It would be preferable to have a model that is capable of describing the path that adjustments might take over time, and in which adjustment costs are explicitly incorporated. Refinements along these lines would likely require a separation of the components of short-run and long-run behavior, as in the structural demand models, but in greater detail than those currently available. As noted throughout, however, these models require considerably richer data than are available for most fuel markets.

Among existing models, the simplest approach uses time-series data to reflect short-run adjustments and cross-section data for long-run adjustments in demand. In both cases the concept of time is suppressed. Comparisons of results obtained from the two data sets are generally consistent with expectations in that short-run elasticities are smaller than long-run elasticities, but the analytical and empirical shortcomings are serious enough to suggest that this approach should be used only for crude approximations when no other alternative is available.

At the next level of complexity, the literature distinguishes between short-run and long-run adjustments using various forms of distributed-lag models. The flow adjustment, stock adjustment, or expectational models of behavior included in this category all reduce to an estimating equation with a lagged dependent variable as an explanatory variable. The coefficient of the lagged variable reflects the speed of adjustment implied by the data, and is used to adjust other coefficients in the model for long-run equilibrium values. The theoretical shortcomings of this procedure have been borne out by the empirical results. The lag coefficients tend to be highly sensitive to minor variations in models or samples and produce elasticity coefficients than can be very unstable, even though they perform well in the usual statistical tests. This approach may be used with some confidence to estimate changes in the rate of utilization of existing capital stocks, but not for longer term adjustments.

A new generation of lag adjustment models is currently under development, as described in Berndt, Morrison, and Watkins (1980), but the procedure has yet to be applied to individual energy products. Several promising features of this new generation of dynamic models address some shortcomings emphasized here. In particular, adjustment costs are explicitly incorporated into the analysis, so that the speed of adjustment becomes endogenously determined and time-oriented. In addition, measures of capital utilization are endogenously determined and influence the path of adjustment over time. However, the dichotomization between short-run and long-run responses common to earlier generations of lag models is retained.

A third and still more complex approach found in existing models emphasizes interfuel substitution relationships in a market share framework. Total energy demand by sector or by end use is modeled separately and then consumption by fuel is estimated as a share of the total. At the sector level, this procedure requires the aggregation of total energy quantities and prices, which raises troublesome questions about estimation errors and the interpretation of results. The models are not based on underlying behavioral hypotheses, and do not lend themselves to the incorporation of additional variables. In particular, the procedure does not facilitate the investigation of capital stock changes, except implicitly through the use of lagged dependent variables. It is also difficult to identify the separate effects of different fuel prices, except through simulation experiments with the model.

Models of market share by end-use category, such as residential space heating, have not been fully exploited because of a lack of data. For this reason, it is not possible to transfer the results obtained from the various end uses to total fuel consumption behavior for each consuming sector. Nevertheless, the available results are instructive in demonstrating the wide variations in demand elasticities by end use, and thus the importance of analyzing specific efficiency standards, use taxes, and similar policy changes at a disaggregated level.

The most complex set of models designed to capture the dynamics of demand is the class of structural demand models that distinguishes between short-run and long-run behavior in separate equations. Short-run variations in utilization rates are derived from a time-series consumption model, while long-run demand is derived from the demand for fuel-using equipment. Several variations of the latter are used, of which the most promising are the discrete-choice models using conditional logit formulations for residential fuel demands. These have worked well when applied to disaggregated data on household consumption and equipment stocks. There are, however, a number of unresolved questions about this technique, including the maintained hypotheses about consumer behavior and the type of data required (see Hartman, 1979). Another variation found in connection with gasoline demand uses automobile demand models, with corresponding adjustments in automobile efficiency combined with changes in vehicle-miles traveled. These models offer a great deal of promise, although further refinements are limited by the quality of available data. It would be useful, also, to update existing results with more recent data.

Determining the level of aggregation

There is considerable evidence of serious aggregation problems in estimating elasticities for groups of consumers. Price elasticities derived from data at finer levels of aggregation tend to be smaller than those obtained from greater aggregative levels. Our observations support the argument that aggregation errors will tend to bias the elasticities upward because of the greater opportunities for variation in consumption that are correlated with, but unrelated to price responses. This conclusion is drawn from measures of long-run elasticities associated with residential and industrial demand. The only comparative evidence available on short-run elasticities pertains to the residential sector and there the differences related to aggregation are not pronounced. There is insufficient comparative evidence on commercial demand to draw a firm conclusion.

There is also evidence that demand models perform better when applied to data at a finer level of aggregation. For example, single-equation models of residential consumption commonly fail to reveal the influence of appliance stocks and appliance prices on fuel consumption behavior when applied to state or national level data. The same type of models, when applied to survey data, tend to show strong and consistent relationships between appliance variables and fuel consumption behavior. Similar findings occur with respect to demographic and climatic variables.

In part, the differences attributed to aggregation bias may arise from multicollinearity, although collinearity can be associated with the level of aggregation. Many variables will exhibit stable trends because of the smoothing effect of aggregation, making it difficult to separate their influences in the same regression. In time-series data, this problem is common among income, demographic, and capital stock variables, and between income and price during periods when the latter is stable. A similar result occurs in cross-section studies, where measures of income and income-related variables (such as appliance saturation and housing characteristics) are collinear. More is said about these relationships in the next section.

Aggregation problems are probably most severe in the industrial sector, where firms are combined even though they produce different products, or the same product with disparate production techniques and energy intensities. There is, however, very little objective evidence about the extent of the biases. Cross-section studies of industrial subclasses, while producing smaller price elasticities than do aggregate time-series models, are themselves subject to considerable bias. The estimates are highly erratic from one year to the next, indicating that changes in the composition of the aggregates may be dominating behavioral responses. Further study at the level of firms is essential to provide reliable evidence on the behavioral side.

The potential estimation bias introduced by aggregation can be seriously misleading, and empirical investigations should be conducted at the finest level of aggregation permitted by available data. Furthermore, when a higher level of generality is required, it is preferable to perform empirical estimation at the micro level and apply an explicit aggregation scheme to obtain the macro results. When there is no alternative to highly aggregated data, analysts and practitioners would be well advised to regard the empirical measures of price elasticities as upper bound values and apply them conservatively.

Separating the determinants of demand

The problems of separating and accurately identifying the contributions of factors affecting energy consumption are common to all energy demand studies. The interdependencies among fuel prices, income (or output) and capital stock make it difficult to sort out their separate influences in regression analysis. The problem is more acute in single-equation models where all the variables enter the same equation as regressors, and in cases where the data are highly aggregated.

In studies of residential demand, the problem is one of separating the influences of price, income, and income-related variables. Price elasticities have been shown to vary among groups of households according to appliance saturation rates, the size of the home, the number of automobiles, and other measures of capital stocks that are related to income. While income and capital stocks are directly related, income and price responses are indirectly linked through capital stocks. Income will also affect price elasticities directly through the budget constraint, since an energy price change has a relatively greater impact on budget decisions among lower income households and forces more immediate adjustments in spending priorities.

It is unusual to find a model that gives statistically significant parameters for price and income, own-prices and competing fuel prices, and for income and capital stock variables, although theory suggests they are all important. Often this is attributed to insufficient variation or collinearity among the explanatory variables. Both problems are frequently alleviated by pooling cross-section and time-series data, while at the same time additional degrees of freedom are gained.

The advantages of pooling data may be more illusory than real, however. First, the combination of time-series and cross-section data introduces confusion in the interpretation of results derived from possibly quite diverse stochastic processes. Second, pooled data introduce other possible sources of bias that can make estimation more cumbersome and less efficient. Finally, there is a collinearity problem with some variables because they are behaviorally interrelated in ways central to understanding the demand process. It is important to explore these relationships explicitly in the model rather than seek to eliminate their symptoms.

In studies of industrial demand, a similar problem of interdependence arises among fuel prices, the rate of output, and capital stocks. Demand models applied to the production sector are analytically capable of handling this type of problem because they are based on the premise of factor substitution, given the level of output and technology. Unfortunately, data limitations force a narrower interpretation of the models by restricting the range of factor substitution, reducing the extent of endogeneity, and virtually eliminating the influence of technology. The role of output is usually retained, but the direct connection with input demand becomes confused in aggregate data because of changes in the composition of output.

Studies of the industrial sector commonly interpret demand elasticities in the narrower sense of factor substitution with a fixed technology. Little is understood about price-induced changes in the composition of output or in technology. We would expect an increase in the relative price of energy to increase the relative price of energy-intensive products (for given technology) and shift consumption toward less energy-intensive products. This shift reduces energy demand, and should be included in the measure of the price elasticity. However, there is at present no evidence that separates price-induced and autonomous changes in output. At the same time, autonomous or price-induced changes in technology may also alter energy input requirements for a given level (and composition) of output, but neither influence can be identified in the analyses of energy demand examined here.

Studies of the commercial sector are both theoretically and empirically inadequate. All of the studies covered here use reduced-form consumption models that duplicate those applied to residential markets, and all but one use data that aggregate over all commercial establishments. There is, as a result, no adequate identification of the influence of activity variables nor distinction by energy intensity.

To summarize, we have some indications of the complexities of residential energy demand, primarily from studies of electricity, but we know very little about commercial and industrial demand beyond simple interfuel substitution relationships. The evidence comes almost entirely from a small subset of studies at the micro level and reinforces the need for additional analyses at the same level in all fuel markets.

Separating supply and demand effects

Several dimensions of the problem of separating the influences of supply and demand in energy markets have been discussed in the preceding chapters. One is the traditional identification problem, where *ex post* observations on price and consumption represent a combination of supply and demand elements that must be separated. The problem is not uniformly troublesome across all markets. Electricity supplied to residential markets, and to a lesser degree natural gas supplied to households, may be reasonably assumed to be perfectly elastic for short periods of time without fear of serious bias problems. A comparison of empirical results obtained from single-equation and multiple-equation models tends to support the *a priori* arguments on this point (after taking into account the characteristics of declining block schedules). Caution is required, however, in extending this assumption to long-run forecasts.

Market conditions are such as to make it dangerous to ignore supply conditions, even for short periods, for fuels consumed by the commercial and industrial sectors, or for petroleum products consumed by any sector. In these cases market prices respond sharply to changes in both supply and demand, making it imperative to treat price as an endogenous variable. Surprisingly few studies in these areas make the effort, and we have little evidence on which to judge the errors introduced into estimation. It is also difficult to model the supply side. Halvorsen makes the most concerted effort with regard to industrial demand for electricity, but his price equation is still a weak representation of hypothesized relationships and the results are poor. No attempts have been made to account for supply effects in electricity demand studies at lower levels of aggregation, and no attempts at all have been made to separate supply effects in models of commercial and industrial demands for other fuels. Among the studies of various petroleum products, a few attempts have been made to incorporate supply in gasoline demand models, though with questionable success.

A second dimension of the supply-demand nexus is the appropriate representation of declining price schedules for electricity and natural gas. The literature has effectively demonstrated the importance of the distinction between marginal and average prices, as elasticities associated with marginal prices are consistently smaller. Still unresolved is the question of which price measure, or combination of price measures, is appropriate in demand analysis. One element of doubt arises from the apparent unimportance of inframarginal rates and fixed charges. It is not clear whether the result is correct, whether it is a product of the measures used, or whether it is due to collinearity among price variables.

Further research on these issues may be of limited usefulness, except as it incorporates some of the changes in electricity pricing structures currently under consideration. The alternatives to traditional declining-block rates being considered or implemented include inverted-block rates, time-of-day pricing, seasonal prices, and other forms. Each variation is likely to have a significant effect on the pattern of electricity use and on the overall volume of consumption. It is doubtful that historical parameter values can be used reliably as the changes become implemented.

A dimension largely ignored in the literature concerns constraints on the supply of energy-using equipment. Equipment often is not immediately available, so that a lag develops between the time a change is desired and when it can be implemented. The lag effect, or induced cost effect, can be important when an energy price change causes a significant shift in demand for capital goods. The shift in consumer preferences for fuel-efficient automobiles provides the most striking recent example of this effect. Because domestic producers did not respond quickly to changes in consumer preferences, the relative price of smaller cars increased, there were fewer options, and longer delivery delays. As a result, the response to gasoline price increases was retarded because improvements in the efficiency of the automobile stock were slowed. As the stock adjusts in time toward a new equilibrium, there remains the problem of correctly associating the observed response with the initial price change. The measurement problem will also become confused with influences working in the opposite direction. For example, as the stock of autos becomes more efficient, and operating costs decline in importance relative to capital costs, the magnitude of the response to an increase in the gasoline price may be expected to decline.

The last major issue raised under the heading of supply-demand interaction is the problem of modeling disequilibrium markets. No study has yet tackled this issue head-on and most ignore it altogether. In studies where the problem is recognized, it is handled by restricting samples to periods where its effects are less evident, or by introducing proxy variables to reflect structural shifts caused by disequilibrium conditions. Neither approach is adequate, and explicit modeling of disequilibrium markets is needed.

This problem is especially serious with respect to markets for natural gas and coal. Natural gas service to commercial and industrial users has been interrupted for periods since 1970, while controls have been placed on residential hookups in many states. The coal market has yet to adjust to environmental regulations, and disincentives created by fuel-cost adjustments and depressed financial positions of utilities slow adjustments. Disequilibrium conditions in markets for petroleum products have occurred sporadically after the advent of price and allocation controls in 1971, with the most serious disturbances evidenced by gasoline shortages in 1974 and 1979. In each case, price-quantity pairs may not fall along a theoretical demand curve, but instead reflect a constrained version dominated by factors other than normal economic incentives. The problem is also widespread because fuel markets are interrelated, so that disequilibrium conditions in one market affect the others to some degree. For example, electricity demand in the industrial sector cannot adjust freely to relative price changes if there are constraints on the use of natural gas and coal. This problem is also acute in analyses of interfuel substitution in electric power generation.

Estimation form and method

The literature employs a wide variety of equation forms and estimation techniques. Indeed, no· readily available tools have been overlooked, though they have not been applied uniformly across fuels and sectors. For example, flexible functional forms have not been used in the models of residential consumption included here, while multinomial logit specifications have not been applied in disaggregated industry models. The linear expenditure system could be applied to fuels other than petroleum, and appliance saturation models may be used in connection with available survey data on residential natural gas consumption. A variable elasticity specification has been employed only with regard to residential electricity consumption, with results sufficiently interesting to warrant experimentation with alternative forms and application to other fuels. In short, researchers have many options to choose from and should select from among them on the basis of the data available and the problem they seek to illuminate.

The standard log-linear form is by far the most common among the studies included here, but its convenience is often thought to be outweighed by the restrictions imposed on elasticities of substitution. The translog form, the most commonly used among the recently developed flexible functional forms, is an appealing alternative because the maintained hypothesis about underlying behavior is less restrictive. However, practical applications of the translog require alternative restrictions that serve to question its superiority. The large number of parameters generated by the models impairs statistical efficiency, limits the number of explanatory variables that can be included, and requires additional restrictions on their behavior. The procedure, as developed so far, assumes that demand is static and that all regressors are exogenous variables. It is particularly troublesome that applications of the translog form do not treat energy as a demand derived from durable goods stocks, but regard durable goods as another separable consumption category. Thus, theoretcial superiority is not retained unambiguously at the practical level.

Regardless of the approach taken, simplifying assumptions are necessary and a certain amount of arbitrariness is involved. The question is still open as to whether simpler equation specifications adequately capture the important characteristics of demand; we have found no obvious evidence that the more complex forms are superior. On the other hand, the simpler forms can be adapted to explore a wide variety of details about demand, and can be implemented in a wider range of models. These features, combined with convenience, argue in favor of the simple log-linear specifications.

Measures of Price Elasticities

Comparative judgments were made in chapters 3–6 about different measures of price elasticities of demand reported for each fuel and consuming factor. These judgments are drawn together in this section to provide a convenient overview of what we regard as the most defensible among alternative measures of price elasticities. These evaluations are, to be sure, highly subjective. While they are perhaps of interest in themselves, we take this opportunity to summarize the principal difficulties in determining reliable estimates in each energy submarket, as well as some considerations involved in choosing among those available.

The criteria used to make comparative judgments among studies is a combination of the estimation technique used and the plausibility of the results obtained. The results from studies that use a structural demand model, that use data at the finest level of aggregation, and that employ estimators which take into account major specification errors are considered more reliable, provided they are also consistent with theory and intuition. In addition, results which reflect significance and consistency across a wider range of behavioral relationships are given preference. Studies which give plausible values for both price and income elasticities, and results which reflect the influence of capital stock and noneconomic variables are preferred.

Only occasionally does the evidence warrant the recommendation of a specific number. For submarkets where no clear preference among results exists, and where there is substantial doubt about their reliability, the estimates are uncertain. This occurs most often when there are no obvious criteria for choosing among widely diverse empirical findings, and occasionally when the findings are in agreement but subject to considerable doubt.

It is necessary to define the context when selecting any value of a price elasticity. The conclusions reported below refer to national markets for each fuel and consuming sector, and relate expected consumption responses to uniform nationwide price increases. They are also premised on markets associated with the economic and institutional conditions of the late 1970s. Consequently, the figures are not necessarily appropriate for subclasses of consumers (say, by region or income), nor can they be used reliably to forecast events after major economic and institutional changes have occurred. Similarly, caution is required in using these elasticities to evaluate government policies if a policy change alters incentive structures in private markets and therefore induces a change in behavioral responses.

In choosing among available figures, it is well to remember that much of the research was conducted using information that is dated by developments in energy markets in the past few years. For this reason, some results are judged unreliable for use in interpreting current and future events. Other results are modified to take into account the expected influence of developments on demand behavior. These modifications are speculative, and introduce another source of uncertainty in the conclusions.

Finally, there is the inevitable range of error that accompanies a statistical estimate. This includes sampling, specification, and forecast errors. In principle, the range of error associated with an estimate can be calculated, but only under specific assumptions about the sample, the behavioral process, and the forecast period. These assumptions are themselves subject to question. Consequently, the magnitude of error is in general unknown and will vary with the choice of assumptions and the specific application of the estimates.

Electricity

Table 7-1 summarizes our conclusions about the estimates for each fuel and consuming sector and compares them with the range of estimates found in the literature (excluding values related to specific regions or end uses). In the case of residential demand for electricity, the evidence is fairly strong that demand is price-inelastic. This conclusion is based on a minority of the studies surveyed, primarily those which analyze data at the household level. While the majority of studies find long-run demand to be elastic, they are composed of reduced-form consumption models fitted with aggregate level data, and are judged less reliable. We also conclude that the consumption response cumulates significantly over time so that the bulk of the total response occurs after the first year.

The elasticity of demand for electricity in the commercial sector is uncertain, owing to the lack of data at a level fine enough to distinguish among commercial activities. Available evidence indicates that demand is highly elastic, though the evidence is, by itself, very weak. Comparative evidence with regard to natural gas demand, though also weak, supports the conclusion that the elasticity exceeds unity (see below). Poor data also obfuscate the results on industrial demand, particularly as the results relate to the short run. There is stronger evidence on the long-run elasticity, because of cross-sectional data, but the most one can say is that it appears to fall somewhere between -0.5 and -1.0. At this level of imprecision, one cannot reasonably speculate about the magnitude of the short-run elasticity.

Natural gas

The estimates of demand elasticities for natural gas are highly uncertain because of a combination of poor data and the confusing effects of disequilibrium markets. Based on studies using household

TABLE 7-1. SUMMARY OF INFORMATION ON PRICE ELASTICITIES OF DEMAND BY FUEL AND SECTOR

Fuel and sector	Estimates in the literature[a]		Conclusions about the estimates	
	Short-run[b]	Long-run[a]	Short-run[b]	Long-run[c]
Electricity				
Residential	-0.06 to -0.49	-0.45 to -1.89	-0.2	-0.70
Commercial	-0.17 to -0.25	-1.00 to -1.60	Uncertain	Uncertain
Industrial	-0.04 to -0.22	-0.51 to -1.82	Uncertain	Between -0.5 and -1.0
Natural gas				
Residential	-0.03 to -0.40	-0.17 to -1.0	-0.10	0.5
Commercial	-0.03 to -0.40	-0.17 to -1.0	Uncertain	Near -1.0
Industrial	-0.07 to -0.21	-0.45 to -1.5	Uncertain	Uncertain
Electric utilities	-0.06	-1.43	-0.06	Uncertain
Gasoline	-0.11 to -0.41	-0.36 to -0.77	-0.2	-0.7 or more elastic
Fuel oil				
Residential	-0.13 to -0.3	-1.1 to -1.76	Uncertain	Uncertain
Commercial	-0.07 to -0.2	-1.1 to -1.76	Uncertain	Uncertain
Industrial	-0.11 to -0.22	-0.8 to -2.82	Uncertain	Uncertain
Electric utilities	-0.10	-1.50	-0.10	Uncertain
Coal (steam)				
Industrial	-0.10 to -0.49	-0.49 to -2.07	Uncertain	Uncertain
Electric utilities	-0.09 to -0.46	-0.67 to -1.15	-0.09	Uncertain

[a]Excluding outlying values related to regions or end uses.
[b]Refers to a response period of one year.
[c]The response period is indefinite, but is generally interpreted to be less than ten years.

survey data, it appears that residential demand has a long-run elasticity of about −0.5. As discussed earlier, survey data in this market may understate the true elasticities. The figure is not adjusted upward because of our related conclusion about residential electricity demand. Virtually all studies support the argument that gas demand is less elastic than that for electricity, given their comparative end uses, so there is little room to adjust this figure upward. All available results on gas consumption are derived in a constrained market and, in view of institutional changes underway in this market, should not be unqualifiedly applied to long-run forecasts of gas demand.

The best evidence available on commercial gas demand places its elasticity near unity. This is based on a single study of survey data from New York state. The other studies, using aggregate data, find demand to be considerably less elastic, but are also less defensible. If commercial gas demand is near unity, then it is plausible that commercial electricity demand is even more elastic, as studies of that market suggest. Estimates in the industrial sector are considered uncertain at all levels, and the same conclusion holds for long-term estimates of gas demand for electricity generation. The short-run elasticity of demand for gas by electric utilities appears to be near zero, but this may be said about all fuels used in this sector because of constraints on fuel substitution with existing equipment.

Gasoline

The literature for gasoline demand is unusually consistent in concluding that the price elasticity is near -0.2 in the short run and -0.7 in the longer term. The long-run figure is probably an overestimate of the true response experienced during the sample periods to which they refer. The studies use, for the most part, single-equation consumption models and highly aggregated data, and both characteristics are in general associated with overestimated price elasticities. In addition, the observation periods predate the rapid increases in gasoline prices and, therefore, will not record the price-induced effects on the efficiency of the automobile stock. Finally, the supply of fuel-efficient automobiles was limited during the sample periods and did not keep pace with changes in consumer preferences once the price of gasoline began to rise.

If the estimates in the literature are evaluated with respect to current market conditions, they are probably closer to the true values and may understate them. The observed shift in consumer preferences for smaller cars, and the corresponding expansion in the supply of smaller cars, support the view that gasoline demand is more responsive to price than is evident in earlier data. We conclude that the long-run elasticity is larger than -0.7, but recognize that it is based on speculation, and should be supported by up-to-date analysis.

Fuel oil

The elasticities for fuel oil demand are uncertain in all categories, owing to poor information about consumption by sector. Among the sectors, better information is available on industrial demand, but even here the results warrant no more than a tentative conclusion that the long-run elasticity may exceed unity. That information is also dated because of changes in the market that affect interfuel substitution.

Coal

The results derived on coal demand are considered to be extremely poor in all categories. The most one can say is that short-run demand by electric utilities, like that for other fuels, has an elasticity close to zero. All other figures should be regarded with suspicion.

To summarize, it is difficult to recommend specific elasticities for many energy submarkets. However, even when elasticities may not be pinpointed (to whatever extent they can ever be pinpointed), the studies do serve to narrow the bounds of uncertainty. We can say conclusively that relative fuel prices are important in energy consumption decisions and should be incorporated in demand analysis. Moreover, we can say that the consumption response will cumulate over time, so that the strength of a price effect should not be judged on the basis of short-term results. The literature also suggests an upper bound on energy price elasticities: energy demand appears to be price-inelastic in all major categories. Elasticities in excess of unity occur only among the least defensible results. Thus, while prices are important, and the consumption response builds over time, one should avoid imputing an elastic response to any fuel price change in any major consuming sector without special justification.

Caveat Emptor

The burden of evaluating the empirical methods and results discussed here ultimately falls on consumers of this information, particularly those who wish to use it in practical applications. It is to this group that we direct some remarks about the inherent limitations of econometric analyses and their implications. These remarks will be obvious to analysts, but they are offered because unrealistic expectations often lead to misunderstandings about the value of information and how it can be used. In broad terms, the limitations on the analyses arise in at least three dimensions: (1) the information base that is available, (2) the concept being investigated, and (3) the intended application of the results.

The data

The quality of the data base places the first constraint on the quantity and quality of information that can be obtained through econometric analysis. Analysts are frequently in the position of trying to make bricks without straw. The more striking gaps in our understanding of demand behavior occur in areas where the data are least adequate. Measures of price elasticities are least reliable for the commercial and industrial sectors, and consumption behavior is least understood when it involves characteristics of capital stocks. There are techniques that may improve understanding in these areas, but they cannot be usefully employed where the data are deficient. Further refinements in econometric methods cannot be expected to overcome the absence of information from which inferences are drawn.

The individual studies in the literature seldom provide a complete appraisal of the data being analyzed, but present their data, methods, and results for readers to evaluate as they choose. Except in extreme cases, this is appropriate because the evaluation ultimately depends on the requirements of the intended application. Therefore, users of the information must understand the deficiencies of the estimates and be aware of possible implications in drawing conclusions from them. Where a variety of data have been used, users are expected to be able to make comparative judgments.

The concept

The concept of a price elasticity of demand also involves inherent limitations on measurement because it embodies a large number of assumptions that must be specified. There is no unique measure of a price elasticity, but an assortment of measures that will vary with the commodity, the consumer, economic conditions, institutional factors, and the time frame. The data used in estimation will incorporate many of these assumptions, while the estimation method will impose additional assumptions on the data in the form of restrictions on parameters. The assumptions will vary with the data set and the estimation technique. One should not be surprised, therefore, to find a wide range of figures purporting to measure the same phenomenon, nor is one figure necessarily more correct than another. Again, it is not possible to say in the abstract which set of assumptions is most appropriate, for the choice depends on the requirements of the specific problem to be addressed.

The burden of the decision again falls on the user. Analysts presumably tailor their choice of data and methods to the intended application, but seldom in published research is there a careful delineation of assumptions and objectives. Often this is because the research is not intended for a specific application, but is offered to different audiences for a variety of reasons. The researcher may be aiming at the demonstration of a new technique, formulation of a new model, or application of new data, without concern for a specific application. Consumers of this information therefore must be as aware as the researchers about the implications of the assumptions in order to choose intelligently among studies and results.

The application

Perhaps the most common application of econometric estimates of elasticity parameters is in forecasting exercises. It follows from the discussion above that the assumptions embodied in the historical analysis should be consistent with those related to the forecast period. The required consistency is not likely to hold in energy markets where major changes are occurring rapidly. Several dimensions of the problem have been discussed throughout this study, including changes in the price range, capital stocks, demographic patterns, consumer tastes, and institutional constraints. In short, major changes in these variables provide the impetus for forecasting their implications, but they also produce changes in the structure of demand that make forecasting all the more difficult. For this reason, it is usually recommended that parameter estimates be continuously updated, not just to avoid obsolescence, but to record the drift in the parameters over time.

It may be delusive to try to determine the drift of behavioral parameters when the events under analysis are responsible for the changes. This is particularly important in forecasting exercises where behavioral parameters are used to evaluate energy policy actions because the policy action may induce changes in behavioral parameters. The structure of an econometric model reflects decision rules of economic agents and policy changes will alter the decision rules [see Lucas (1976)]. The implication is that traditional demand models may be appropriate for short-term forecasting purposes, because the impact of policy change on consumption behavior will take time, but inappropriate for evaluating the longer term implications of policy decisions. This concern is relevant for all major energy proposals, including utility rate reform, consumption taxes, energy-related tax credits, oil import controls, fuel efficiency standards, and fuel consumption regulations.

It is beyond the capability of existing econometric models of energy demand to incorporate the effect of policy decisions on behavioral parameters. This would require estimates of behavioral parameters that vary systematically with both economic activity and policy variables. There is little hope that the structural changes that might be contemplated for energy can be estimated from past data.

The implication of these remarks for practitioners is clear. They are expected to make judgments about forecast periods relative to historical periods and about potential structural changes in the demand model they wish to apply. There is, moreover, no specific guidance in the empirical literature to assist in making these judgments. There is at best indirect evidence on the stability of parameters associated with different sample periods and different economic conditions.

References

Acton, J. P., B. M. Mitchell, and R. S. Mowill. 1976. *Residential Demand for Electricity in Los Angeles: An Econometric Study of Disaggregated Data.* Report R-1899-NSF (Santa Monica, Calif., Rand Corp.).

Adams, F. G., H. Graham, and J. M. Griffin. 1974. *Demand Elasticities for Gasoline: Another View.* Discussion Paper no. 279 (Philadelphia, Pa., University of Pennsylvania, Economic Research Unit).

Allen, R. G. D. 1938. *Mathematical Analysis for Economists* (London, Macmillan).

———. 1960. *Mathematical Economics* (London, Macmillan).

Almon, Shirley. 1965. "The Distributed Lag Between Capital Appropriations and Expenditures," *Econometrica* vol. 33, no. 1 (January) pp. 178–196.

Alt, Christopher, Anthony Bopp, and George Lady. 1976. "Short-Term Forecasts of Energy Supply and Demand," in A. Bradley Askin and John Kraft, eds., *Econometric Dimensions of Energy Demand and Supply* (Lexington, Mass., D. C. Heath).

Anderson, Kent P. 1971. *Toward Econometric Estimation of Industrial Energy Demand: An Experimental Application to the Primary Metals Industry.* Report R-719-NSF (Santa Monica, Calif., Rand Corp.).

———. 1973. *Residential Energy Use: An Econometric Analysis.* Report R-1296-NSF (Santa Monica, Calif., Rand Corp.).

———. 1974. *The Price Elasticity of Residential Energy Use.* Report P-5180 (Santa Monica, Calif., Rand Corp.).

Archibald, Robert, and Robert Gillingham. 1978. *Two Studies of Consumer Demand for Gasoline.* BLS Working Paper 83 (Washington, D.C., U.S. Department of Labor).

Asher, Harold, and Rudolph Habermann, Jr. 1978. *Analysis of Recent Fluctuations in Electricity Consumption.* Report CFESR-77-3 (Washington, D.C., General Electric Co., Center for Energy Systems).

Askin, A. Bradley, and John Kraft. 1976. *Econometric Dimensions of Energy Demand and Supply* (Lexington, Mass., D. C. Heath).

Atkinson, Scott, and Robert Halvorsen. 1976a. "Demand for Fossil Fuels by Electric Utilities," in A. Bradley Askin and John Kraft, eds., *Econometric Dimensions of Energy Demand and Supply* (Lexington, Mass., D. C. Heath).

———, and ———. 1976b. "Interfuel Substitution in Steam Electric Power Generation," *Journal of Political Economy* vol. 84, no. 5, pp. 959–978.

Averch, Harvey, and Leland L. Johnson. 1962. "Behavior of the Firm Under Regulatory Constraint," *American Economic Review* vol. 52, no. 5 (December) pp. 1052–1069.

Balestra, Pietro. 1967. *The Demand for Natural Gas in the United States* (Amsterdam, North-Holland).

————, and Marc Nerlove. 1966. "Pooling Cross Section and Time Series Data in the Estimation of a Dynamic Model: The Demand for Natural Gas," *Econometrica* vol. 34, no. 3 (July) pp. 585–612.

Barten, A. P. 1970. "Reflexions sur le construction d'un systeme empirique des fonctions de demande," *Cahiers du Seminaire d'Econometrice* no. 12.

Barzel, Yoram. 1964. "The Production Function and Technical Change in the Steam Power Industry," *Journal of Political Economy* vol. 72 (April) pp. 133–150.

Baughman, Martin, and Paul Joskow. 1975. *Energy Consumption and Fuel Choice by Residential and Commercial Consumers in the United States.* Report MIT-EL-75-024 (Cambridge, Mass., Massachusetts Institute of Technology Energy Laboratory).

————, and Frederick Zerhoot. 1975. *Interfuel Substitution in the Consumption of Energy in the United States, Part II: Industrial Sector.* Report MIT-EL-75-007 (Cambridge, Mass., Massachusetts Institute of Technology Energy Laboratory).

Berndt, Ernst R., and David O. Wood. 1975. "Technology, Prices, and the Derived Demand for Energy," *The Review of Economics and Statistics* vol. 57, no. 3 (August) pp. 259–268.

————, Melvin A. Fuss, and Leonard Waverman. 1977. *Dynamic Models of the Industrial Demand for Energy.* Report EPRI EA-580 (Palo Alto, Calif., Electric Power Research Institute).

————, and G. C. Watkins. 1977. "Demand for Natural Gas: Residential and Commercial Markets in Ontario and British Columbia," *Canadian Journal of Economics* vol. X, no. 1 (February) pp. 97–111.

————, C. J. Morrison, and G. C. Watkins. 1980. "Dynamic Models of Energy Demand: An Assessment and Comparison." Research Paper no. 49 (Vancouver, University of British Columbia).

Bohi, Douglas R., and Milton Russell. 1978. *Limiting Oil Imports: An Economic History and Analysis* (Baltimore, Md., Johns Hopkins University Press for Resources for the Future).

Brown, Alan, and Angus Deaton. 1972. "Surveys in Applied Economics: Models of Consumer Behavior," *The Economic Journal* vol. 82, no. 328 (December) pp. 1145–1236.

Burright, Burke K., and John H. Enns. 1975. *Econometric Models of the Demand for Motor Fuel.* Report R-1561-NSF/FEA (Santa Monica, Calif., Rand Corp.).

Carlson, M. T. 1974. "The 1972-73 Consumer Expenditure Survey," *Monthly Labor Review* vol. 97, no. 12 (December) pp. 16–23.

Cato, Darriel, Mark Rodekohr, and James Sweeney. 1976. "The Capital Stock Adjustment Process and the Demand for Gasoline: A Market-Share Approach," in A. Bradley Askin and John Kraft, eds., *Econometric Dimensions of Energy Demand and Supply* (Lexington, Mass., D. C. Heath).

Chang, Hui S., and Wen S. Chern. 1978. "A Study in Electricity Demand and Variation in the Price Elasticity of Demand for Manufacturing Industries." Draft (Oak Ridge, Tenn., Oak Ridge National Laboratory).

Charles River Associates, Inc. (CRA). 1976. *Long-Range Forecasting Properties of State-of-the-Art Models of Demand for Electric Energy.* Report EA-221 (Palo Alto, Calif., Electric Power Research Institute).

Chase Econometrics, Inc. 1974. *The Effect of Tax and Regulatory Alternatives on Car Sales and Gasoline Consumption.* Prepared for the U. S. Council on Environmental Quality, Contract No. EQ4AC004.

Chern, Wen S. 1976. *Energy Demand and Interfuel Substitution in the Combined Residential and Commercial Sector.* Report RM-5557 (Oak Ridge, Tenn., Oak Ridge National Laboratory).

————, and William Lin. 1976. "Energy Demand for Space Heating: An Econometric Analysis," in American Statistical Association, *1976 Proceedings of the Business and Economics Section,* pp. 250–254.

Chow, Gregory. 1957. *The Demand for Automobiles in the United States* (Amsterdam, North-Holland).

Christensen, L. R., and W. H. Greene. 1976. "Economies of Scale in U.S. Electric Power Generation," *Journal of Political Economy* vol. 84, part 1 (July/August) pp. 655–676.

————, Dale Jorgenson, and Lawrence Lau. 1973. "Transcendental Logarithmic Production Frontiers," *The American Economic Review* vol. 51, no. 1 (February) pp. 28–45.

————, ————, and ————. 1975. "Transcendental Logarithmic Utility Functions," *The American Economic Review* vol. 65, no. 3 (June) pp. 367–383.

Cohn, Steve, Eric Hirst, and Jerry Jackson. 1977. *Econometric Analyses of Household Fuel Demands.* Report ORNL/CON-7 (Oak Ridge, Tenn., Oak Ridge National Laboratory).

Data Resources, Inc. 1973. *A Study of the Quarterly Demand for Gasoline and Impacts of Alternative Gasoline Taxes.* Prepared for the Environmental Protection Agency and the Council on Environmental Quality.

Deaton, A. S. 1974. "A Reconsideration of the Empirical Implications of Additive Preferences," *The Economic Journal* vol. 84 (June) pp. 338–348.

Department of Energy (DOE). 1978. *Draft Documentation Report on the Regional Demand Forecasting Model, 1977 Version.* Prepared by Synergy, Inc., Washington, D.C.

Dhrymes, Phoebus, and Mordechai Kurz. 1964. "Technology and Scale in Electricity Generation," *Econometrica* vol. 32, no. 3 (July) pp. 287–315.

Diewert, W. E. 1974. "Applications of Duality Theory," in M. D. Intriligator and D. A. Kendrick, eds., *Frontiers of Quantitative Economics,* volume 2 (Amsterdam, North-Holland).

Energy Modeling Forum (EMF). 1978. *Coal in Transition: 1980–2000.* EMF Report 2, volumes 1 and 2 (Stanford, Calif., Stanford University).

Erickson, Edward, Robert Spann, and Robert Ciliano. 1973. "Substitution and Usage in Energy Demand: An Econometric Estimation of Long-Run and Short-Run Effects," in Milton Searl, ed., *Energy Modeling* (Washington, D.C., Resources for the Future).

Farrell, M. J. 1954. "The Demand for Motor Cars in the United States," *Journal of the Royal Statistical Society,* series A, vol. 117, no. 2 (February) pp. 171–193.

Federal Energy Administration (FEA). 1976. *National Energy Outlook* (Washington, D.C., GPO).

———. 1974. *Project Independence Report* (Washington, D.C., GPO).

Fisher, Franklin M. 1966. *The Identification Problem in Econometrics* (New York, McGraw-Hill).

———, and Carl Kaysen. 1962. *A Study in Econometrics: The Demand for Electricity in the United States* (Amsterdam, North-Holland).

Fuss, Melvin A. 1971. "Factor Substitution in Electricity Generation: A Test of the Putty-Clay Hypothesis." Research Discussion Paper no. 185 (Cambridge, Mass., Harvard Institute of Economic Research).

Galatin, Malcolm. 1968. *Economies of Scale and Technological Changes in Thermal Power Generation* (Amsterdam, North-Holland).

Gill, G. S., and G. S. Maddala. 1976. "Residential Demand for Electricity in the TVA Area: An Analysis of Structural Change," in American Statistical Association, *1976 Proceedings of the Business and Economic Statistics Section,* pp. 315–319.

Gorman, W. M. 1953. "Community Preference Fields," *Econometrica* vol. 21 (January).

———. 1959. "Separable Utility and Aggregation." *Econometrica* vol. 27, no. 3 (July) pp. 469–481.

Greene, David L. 1978. *Econometric Analysis of the Demand for Gasoline at the State Level.* Report ORNL/TM-6326 (Oak Ridge, Tenn., Oak Ridge National Laboratory).

Griffin, James M. 1974. "The Effects of Higher Prices on Electricity Consumption," *The Bell Journal of Economics and Management Science* vol. 5, no. 2 (Autumn) pp. 515–539.

Griliches, Zvi, ed. 1971. *Price Indexes and Quality Change* (Cambridge, Mass., Harvard University Press).

Halvorsen, Robert. 1975. "Residential Demand for Electric Energy," *Review of Economics and Statistics* vol. 57, no. 1 (February) pp. 12–18.

———. 1978. *Econometric Models of U.S. Energy Demand* (Lexington, Mass., D. C. Heath).

Hartman, Raymond S. 1978. *A Critical Review of Single Fuel and Interfuel Substitution Residential Energy Demand Models.* Report MIT-EL-78-003 (Cambridge, Mass., Massachusetts Institute of Technology Energy Laboratory).

Hewlett, James G. 1977. "Changing Patterns of Households' Consumption of Energy Commodities," in American Statistical Association, *1977 Proceedings of the Business and Economic Statistics Section* (Part 1) pp. 99–108.

Hicks, J. R. 1939. *Value and Capital* (Oxford, Oxford University Press, reprinted 1974).

Houthakker, H. S. 1951. "Electricity Tariffs in Theory and Practice," *The Economic Journal* vol. 61, no. 241 (March) pp. 1–25.

———, and Lester D. Taylor, 1970. *Consumer Demand in the United States: Analyses and Projections* (Cambridge, Mass., Harvard University Press).

———, Philip K. Verleger, Jr., and Dennis Sheehan. 1974. "Dynamic Demand Analyses for Gasoline and Residential Electricity," *American Journal of Agricultural Economics* vol. 56, no. 2 (May) pp. 412–418.

Iulo, William. 1961. *Electric Utilities: Costs and Performance* (Pullman, Wash., Washington State University Press).

Johnson, Terry R. 1978. "Aggregations and the Demand for New and Used Automobiles," *Review of Economic Studies* vol. 45, no. 2 (June) pp. 311–327.

Johnston, J. 1972. *Econometric Methods* (New York, McGraw-Hill).

Khazzoom, J. Daniel. 1977. "An Application of the Concepts of Free and Captive Demand to the Estimating and Simulating of Energy Demand in Canada," in William D. Nordhaus, ed., *International Studies of the Demand for Energy* (Amsterdam, North-Holland).

Komiya, Ryutaro. 1962. "Technological Progress and the Production Function in the United States Steam Power Industry," *The Review of Economics and Statistics* vol. 44, no. 2 (May) pp. 156–166.

Kouris, George J. 1978. "Price Sensitivity of Petrol Consumption and Some Policy Indications: The Case of the EEC," *Energy Policy* vol. 6, no. 3 (September) pp. 209–216.

Koyck, L. M. 1954. *Distributed Lags and Investment Analysis* (Amsterdam, North-Holland).

Kuh, Edwin. 1976. "Preliminary Observations on the Stability of the Translog Production Function: in J. D. Khazzoom, ed., *Proceedings of the Workshop on Modeling the Interrelationships Between the Energy Sector and the General Economy.* Special Report no. 45, chap. 16 (Palo Alto, Calif., Electric Power Research Institute).

Lacy, A. W., and D. R. Street. 1975. "A Single Firm Analysis of the Residential Demand for Electricity." (Auburn, Alabama, University of Alabama, Department of Economics).

Lawrence, A. G. 1972. "Inter-Fuel Substitution: Steam Electric Generation's Demand for Fuels." Research Discussion Paper no. 8 (Washington, D.C., U.S. Bureau of Labor Statistics).

Leontief, Wassily. 1936. "Composite Commodities and the Problem of Index Numbers," *Econometrica* vol. 4.

Ling, Suilin. 1964. *Economies of Scale in the Steam-Electric Power Generating Industry: An Analytical Approach* (Amsterdam, North-Holland).

Lomax, K. S. 1952. "Cost Curves for Electricity Generation," *Econometrica* vol. 19, no. 74 (May) pp. 193–197.

Lucas, Robert E., Jr. 1976. "Econometric Policy Evaluation: A Critique," in Karl Brunner and Allan H. Meltzer, eds., *The Phillips Curve and Labor Markets*; supplementary series to the *Journal of Monetary Economics,* vol. 1 (Amsterdam, North-Holland).

MacAvoy, Paul, and Robert S. Pindyck. 1973. "Alternative Regulatory Policies for Dealing with the Natural Gas Shortage," *The Bell Journal of Economics and Management Science* vol. 4, no. 2 (Autumn) pp. 454–498.

Malinvaud, Edmund. 1972. *Lectures on Microeconomic Theory* (Amsterdam, North-Holland).

McFadden, Daniel. 1964. "Notes on the Estimation of the Elasticity of Substitution." Working Paper no. 57 (Berkeley, Calif., University of California Institute of Business and Economic Research).

———, and Carlos Puig. 1975. "An Econometric Model of the Demand for Electricity," in *Economic Impact of Water Pollution Control on the Steam Electric Industry*. Report EED-12 (Washington, D.C., Teknekron, Inc.).

———, ———, and Daniel Kirshner. 1977. "Determinants of the Long-Run Demand for Electricity," in American Statistical Association, *1977 Proceedings of the Business and Economic Statistics Section* (Part 2) pp. 109–117.

McGillivray, R. G. 1976. "Gasoline Use by Automobiles," in *Transportation Energy Conservation and Demand* (Washington, D.C., National Academy of Sciences, National Research Council) pp. 45–56.

Moore, Thomas G. 1970. "The Effectiveness of Regulation of Electric Utility Prices," *Southern Economic Journal* vol. 36, no. 4 (April) pp. 365–375.

Mount, T. D., L. D. Chapman, and T. J. Tyrrell. 1973. *Electricity Demand in the United States: An Econometric Analysis*. Report ORNL-NSF-EP-49 (Oak Ridge, Tenn., Oak Ridge National Laboratory).

National Economic Research Associates, Inc. (NERA). 1977. *Consideration of the Price Elasticity of Demand for Electricity: Topic 2*. Prepared by NERA, New York, N.Y.

Nerlove, Marc. 1968. "Returns to Scale in Electricity Supply," in Arnold Zellner, ed., *Readings in Economic Statistics and Econometrics* (Boston, Little, Brown) pp. 409–439.

———. 1971. "Further Evidence on the Estimation of Dynamic Economic Relations from a Time Series of Cross Sections," *Econometrica* vol. 39, no. 2 (March) pp. 359–382.

Newman, D. K., and D. Day. 1975. *The American Energy Consumer* (Cambridge, Mass., Ballinger).

Olson, Charles E., Franklin E. Robeson, and John A. Neri. 1979. *The Demand for Gas: A Study of Residential and Commercial User Characteristics in New York State*. A report to the New York Gas Group, prepared by H. Zinder and Associates, Washington, D.C.

Pearce, I. F. 1964. *A Contribution to Demand Analysis* (Oxford, Oxford University Press).

Phlips, Louis. 1972. "A Dynamic Version of the Linear Expenditure Model," *Review of Economics and Statistics* vol. 54, no. 4 (November) pp. 450–458.

Prais, S. J., and H. S. Houthakker. 1955. *The Analysis of Family Budgets* (Cambridge, Cambridge University Press).

Ramsey, J. B., R. Rasche, and B. Allen. 1975. "An Analysis of the Private and Commercial Demand for Gasoline," *Review of Economics and Statistics* vol. 57, no. 4 (November) pp. 502–507.

Reddy, Nallapu N. 1974. "The Demand for Coal in the United States: An Econometric Analysis," in *Proceedings of the Council of Economics,* AIME Annual Meeting, Dallas, Texas.

Resek, Robert W. and Robert K. Springer. 1977. "Time Lags in the Demand for Gasoline: Effects of a Durable Good," in American Statistical Association, *1977 Proceedings of the Business and Economic Statistics Section* (Part 2) pp. 476–480.

Samuelson, Paul A. 1965. *Foundations of Economic Analysis* (New York, Atheneum).

———. 1974. "Complementarity: An Essay on the 40th Anniversary of the Hicks-Allen Revolution in Demand Theory," *Journal of Economic Literature* vol. 12, no. 4 (December) pp. 1255–1289.

Schneider, A. M. 1977. "Elasticity of Demand for Gasoline Since the 1973 Oil Embargo," *Energy: The International Journal* vol. 2, no. 1 (March) pp. 45–52.

Schultz, Henry. 1938. *The Theory and Measurement of Demand* (Chicago, University of Chicago Press).

Schurr, Sam H., Joel Darmstadter, Harry Perry, William Ramsay, and Milton Russell. 1979. *Energy in America's Future: The Choices Before Us* (Baltimore, Md., Johns Hopkins University Press for Resources for the Future).

Stanford Research Institute. 1972. *Patterns of Energy Consumption in the United States* (Washington, D.C., GPO).

Strotz, Robert H. 1959. "The Utility Tree—A Correction and Further Appraisal," *Econometrica* vol. 27, no. 3 (July) pp. 482–488.

Sweeney, James. 1975. "Passenger Use of Gasoline." Mimeo (Washington, D.C., Federal Energy Administration).

Taylor, L. D. 1975. "The Demand for Electricity: A Survey," *The Bell Journal of Economics and Management Science* vol. 6, no. 1 (Spring) pp. 74–110.

———. 1977. "The Demand for Energy: A Survey of Price and Income Elasticities," in William D. Nordhaus, ed., *International Studies of the Demand for Energy* (Amsterdam, North-Holland).

———, G. R. Blattenberger, and P. K. Verleger, Jr. 1977. *The Residential Demand for Energy*, vol. 1. Report EA-235 (Palo Alto, Calif., Electric Power Research Institute).

Theil, Henri. 1971. *Principles of Econometrics* (New York, Wiley).

Uri, Noel D. 1976. "Short-Run Variations in the Demand for Electrical Energy," in American Statistical Association, *1976 Proceedings of the Business and Economic Statistics Section,* pp. 618–621.

———. 1978. "Regional Interfuel Substitution by Electric Companies: The Short-Term Prospects," *Annals of Regional Science* vol. 12, no. 2 (July) pp. 4–15.

Verleger, Philip K., Jr., and Florinda Iascone. 1977. *The Residential Demand*

for Energy: Estimates of Residential Stocks of Energy Using Capital. Report
EA-235 (Palo Alto, Calif., Electric Power Research Institute).

————, and Dennis Sheehan. 1976. "A Study of the Demand for Gasoline," in
Dale Jorgenson, ed., *Econometric Studies of U.S. Energy Policy*
(Amsterdam, North-Holland).

Wills, J. 1977. *Residential Demand For Electricity in Massachusetts.* Working
Paper no. MIT-EL-77-016WP (Cambridge, Mass., Massachusetts Institute
of Technology).

Wilson, John W. 1971. "Residential Demand for Electricity," *The Quarterly
Review of Economics and Business* vol. 11, no. 1 (Spring) pp. 7–19.

————. 1974. "Electricity Consumption: Supply Requirements, Demand
Elasticity and Rate Design," *American Journal of Agricultural Economics*
vol. 56, no. 2 (May) pp. 419–427.

Wykoff, F. C. 1973. "A User Cost Approach to New Automobile Purchases,"
Review of Economic Studies vol. 40, no. 123 (July) pp. 377–390.

Index

Acton, J. P., 65, 66
Adams, F. G., 119
Aggregation of consumer demand, 4
  for all fuels, 109–110
  for coal, 140
  by commodity group, 29
  compared with individual consumer demand, 11–12
  for electricity: commercial, 81; industrial, 83, 85; residential, 56, 62–65, 67–69, 70–72, 74–77
  estimation problems relating to, 148, 149–150
  explanation of, 11–12, 28–29
  for gasoline, 116, 120
  by households, 36
  by individual demand functions, 30
  levels of, 30–32
  for natural gas, 96
  samples for, 31
  sector differences in, 28
Air pollution regulations, coal demand and, 44–45, 136–138, 140
Allen, B., 118, 119
Allen, R. G. D., 14
Almon, Shirley, 20, 67, 83
Alt, Christopher, 121, 129
American Petroleum Institute (API), 118, 120
Anderson, Kent P., 25, 62, 73, 85, 88, 89, 104, 109, 129, 131, 133, 142, 144
API. See American Petroleum Institute
Appliances. See Household appliances
Archibald, Robert, 116, 119
Atkinson, Scott, 49, 50, 110, 112, 133, 140
Automobiles
  demand for: by fuel efficiency, 123–124; market share models for, 124–125; structural models for, 26
  elasticity of ownership of, 123
  gasoline as percent of operating costs of, 115
  supply of small, fuel-efficient, 42–43
Averch, Harvey, 63

Balestra, Pietro, 40, 44, 96, 100–102
Barten, A. P., 29
Baughman, Martin, 17, 71, 83, 107, 131, 142
Berndt, Ernst R., 49, 89, 102, 103, 148
Blattenberger, G. R., 25, 36, 75, 103, 129
Bopp, Anthony, 121, 129
Brown, Alan, 29, 30
Bureau of Census, Consumer Expenditure Survey, 116, 119
Burright, Burke K., 26, 123, 125

Capital stock, of energy-using equipment
  adequacy of data on, 17
  effect on energy supply, 42–43
  in reduced-form models, 16–17
  relation between fuel prices and, 14–15
  in structural demand models, 24–25
Cato, Darriel, 26, 116, 124
Census of Manufactures, 89
Chang, Hui S., 91
Chapman, L. D., 68, 82
Charles River Associates (CRA), 62, 63, 68, 85, 88
Chase Econometrics, Inc., 124
Chern, Wen S., 17, 71, 72, 91, 129
Christensen, L. R., 48
Ciliano, Robert, 73, 104
Clean air Act of 1967, 136
Clean Air Act Amendments of 1977, 136
Coal
  cross-price elasticity with fuel oil, 133
  demand for: deficiencies in studies of, 144; for electricity generation, 135, 137, 140–142; environmental regulations and, 136–138; interfuel substitution and, 137, 139, 141; by manufacturing, 142, 144; technological changes and, 135–136
  disequilibrium in market for, 44–45, 138, 155
  measurement of market price for, 139–140
  price elasticity of, 137, 141, 142, 144, 161; long-run versus short-run, 137, 141, 161
  steam versus coking, 135, 142
Cohn, Steve, 67, 96, 103, 129
Commercial sector
  aggregation of fuel consumption in, 28, 30, 31
  data on electricity consumption in, 32
  electricity demand by, 79–82, 158
  energy demand studies, 152
  fuel oil demand by, 128–129, 131
  measurement of fuel consumption in, 16
  natural gas demand by, 93–105
  price-quantity interdependence for electricity and natural gas in, 40
Composite commodity theorem, 29
Conditional logit model, 17, 26
Consumer demand for energy
  income and, 1, 8
  marginal utility and, 8, 10
  market demand functions to estimate, 11–12
  under perfect competition, 10
Cost functions, factor prices and, 9, 10
  see also Unit cost function
CRA. See Charles River Associates

Cross-price elasticity
Coal, 141–143
  electricity, 73, 77, 78
  explanation of, 13–14
  fuel oil, 133
  functional form for, 51
  natural gas, 104, 106, 109, 111, 112
  in reduced-form consumption models, 22
  regional differences in, 111
Cross-section studies, 17–18
  bias in, 150
  for electricity demand, 61, 67–68, 88–89
  for natural gas demand, 96, 112

Data Resources, Inc., 120
Deaton, Angus, 29, 30, 48, 62
Diesel fuel, demand for, 127–128
Diewert, W. E., 22
Distributed-lag model, 20–21, 67, 147–148
DOE. See Energy, Department of
Durbin-Watson statistic, 20

Elasticity of demand
  definitions of, 12–14
  functional forms for, 45–52
  see also Cross-price elasticity; Income elastici-
    ty; Own-price elasticity; Price elasticity;
    Substitution, elasticity of interfuel
Electricity
  commercial demand for, 79–82, 158
  consumption of, by sector, 31, 32
  cross-elasticity of demand relationships, 13
  cross-sectional differences in demand for, 62,
    66–67, 68, 78, 89–90
  identification problem and, 63, 64, 153
  industrial demand for: aggregation of data
    for, 83, 85; deficiencies in studies of, 91;
    locational effects on, 88–89; price elastic-
    ity of, 83, 85, 87–91; by-product classes,
    85, 87; technology and, 91; unit cost
    function for, 89; value added in, 87, 88,
    89
  interfuel substitution in generation of, 49
  price-quantity interdependence for, 35, 39–41
  prices: appliance utilization rate and, 65,
    75–76; average, 56, 61, 63, 64; marginal,
    56, 63, 64, 65, 66, 69; regulations effect
    on, 63
  residential demand for: aggregation of data
    for, 56, 62–65, 67–69, 70–72; comparison
    of studies on, 55–61; deficiencies in
    studies of, 79; dynamic consumption
    models for, 67–70; fuel share models for,
    71–74; income elasticity of, 56, 61, 62, 73,
    78–79; price elasticity of, 56, 60, 62–66,
    69–70, 73–75, 77–79, 158; static con-
    sumption models for, 61–66; structural
    demand models for, 74–77
Electric utilities
  coal demand by, 140–142
  natural gas demand by, 105, 106
Energy consumption
  income and price and, 53

reduced-form models to estimate, 15–21
  by sector, 16–17
Energy demand, 2, 7
  aggregation of data to measure, 28–33
  capital stock and, 14–15
  consumer versus producer, 8–11
  cross-elasticity relationships, 13–14
  dynamics of, 4, 14–15; estimation problems
    relating to, 147–149; reduced-form con-
    sumption model for, 15–23, 28; structural
    demand model for, 23–27
  econometric studies of: applied to forecast-
    ing, 3–4, 163–164; assumptions inherent
    in, 162–163; choice of, 3; estimating
    options in 155–156; quality of data for,
    162; reliability of, 3, 146
  fuel-using equipment, supply effect on, 41–43
  individual demand functions to estimate, 8–11
  market demand functions to estimate, 11–12
  price influences separated from other deter-
    minants of, 52–53, 151–152
  separation of supply effects from, 153–155
  static versus dynamic analysis of, 11, 53
  structural models for, 23–27
  time-oriented, 15
  see also Aggregation of consumer demand;
    Elasticity of demand; Individual consum-
    er demand
Energy, Department of (DOE), 17, 71, 82, 96,
  104, 107, 127, 131, 144
Energy supply
  assumed perfect elasticity of, 34
  fuel-using equipment supply and, 41–43
  identification problem relating to analysis of,
    33–34
  interdependence between price and, 35–41
  separation of demand effects from, 153–155
Enns, John H., 26, 123, 125
Equilibrium market, 4
  dynamic versus static, 11
  long-run vesus short-run adjustments for, 17
  regulations effect on, 34, 43–45
Erickson, Edward, 73, 104
European Economic community, gasoline consumption data for, 122

Factors of production. See Inputs
Federal Highway Administration (FHWA),
  118, 120
Federal Power Commission, 133
FHWA. See Federal Highway Administration
Fisher, Franklin M., 24–25, 41, 61, 85, 87, 88, 89
Forecasting, econometric studies for, 3–4, 163–
  164
Fuel oil
  consumption, by sector, 31–32
  deficiencies in demand studies of, 131, 134
  industrial demand for: by electric utilities,
    133–134; by primary metals industry,
    131, 133
  interfuel substitution with, 129, 131, 133, 134
  residential and commercial demand for,
    128–129, 131; price and income elasticity
    of, 129, 160–161

Fuel-using equipment
  relation of energy demand and demand for,
    14–15
  supply of, 41–43
Fuss, Melvin A., 49

Gasoline
  data on, 32, 118
  demand for: automobile demand and, 123–
    125, 149; cross-elasticity relationships,
    13; deficiencies in studies of, 126–127;
    dynamic consumption models for, 120–
    122; and fuel-efficient cars, 26–27, 43,
    123–124; income elasticity of, 116, 118,
    120, 122, 123, 126–127; price elasticity of,
    116, 120–121, 123, 125, 126–127, 160;
    stability in, 122; static consumption
    models for, 118–120; structural models
    for, 26–27, 123–125
  as percent of automobile operating costs, 115
Gill, G. S., 68
Gillingham, Robert, 116, 119
Gorman, W. M., 29, 30
Graham, H., 119
Greene, David L., 118, 119
Griffin, James M., 67, 83, 119

Halvorsen, Robert, 25, 37, 38, 49, 50, 62, 63, 64,
    65, 81, 83, 85, 89, 110, 112, 131, 133, 140,
    141, 144
Hartman, Raymond S., 149
Hewlett, James G., 66, 96
Hicks, J. R., 29
Hirst, Eric, 67, 96, 103, 129
Household appliances
  deficiencies in data on, 24–25
  electricity use by, 24–26, 65, 66, 73, 74–78
  fuel oil use by, 129
  natural gas use by, 100–102, 104
Houthakker, H. S., 19, 35, 67, 120

Iascone, Florinda, 75
Identification, in supply and demand analysis
  for electricity, 63, 64, 153–154
  estimation problems in, 33–34, 151
  and interdependence between price and
    quantity, 39–41, 153
  and market equilibrium, 43–45
  for natural gas, 106, 154
  by sector, 152
  supply of equipment and, 42, 43
Income
  and commercial demand for electricity, 81
  effect on price elasticity, 1, 8, 46–47, 48, 53,
    151
  and residential demand for electricity, 56, 61,
    62, 66, 73
  and total fuel consumption, 53, 79
Income elasticity
  criteria for evaluating studies on, 157
  electricity, 56, 61, 62, 66, 69, 73
  fuel oil, 129
  functional form for, 46
  gasoline, 116, 118, 120, 122, 123, 126–127

nongasoline transportation fuels, 127–128
Individual consumer demand, 8–11
  elasticity, 29
  for electricity, 56, 66, 78
  for gasoline, 119
  for natural gas, 93
  sectoral differences in, 28
Industrial sector
  aggregation of fuel consumption in, 28, 30, 31
  coal demand by, 142–144
  data on electricity consumption in, 32
  electricity demand by, 82–92
  energy demand studies for, 152
  fuel oil demand by, 131–134
  measurement of fuel consumption in, 16
  natural gas demand by, 105–113
  price-quantity interdependence for electricity
    and natural gas in, 40
Inputs
  energy: demand for, 8–9, 22; prices and use
    of, 10; in reduced-form consumption
    model, 21–22
  production: elasticities of substitution among,
    48, 50–51; least-cost combination of, 10
Institutional factors, affecting energy markets,
    3, 44–45, 138–139, 157

Jackson, Jerry, 67, 96, 103, 129
Johnson, Leland L., 63
Jorgenson, Dale, 48
Joskow, Paul, 17, 71

Kaysen, Carl, 25–25, 41, 61, 85, 87, 88, 89
Khazzoom, J. Daniel, 103
Kirshner, Daniel, 26, 66, 75
Kouris, George J., 121, 122
Koyck, L. M., 18, 19
Kuh, Edwin, 49, 51

Lady, George, 121, 129
Lag-adjustment model, 18–20, 67
Lau, Lawrence, 48
Lawrence, A. G., 110
Leontieff, Wassily, 29
Linear model, 17, 155
Lin, William, 73
Logit model, of appliance saturation rates, 76
Log-linear model, 17, 156
  for electricity consumption, 62, 64, 68, 69
Lucas, Robert E. Jr., 164

MacAvoy, Paul, 102
McFadden, Daniel, 26, 63, 64, 66, 75
McGillivray, R. G., 121
Maddala, G. S., 68
Manufacturing
  coal demand by, 142, 144
  electricity demand by, 85
  fuel oil demand by, 131, 133
  natural gas demand by, 105–106, 107, 109
Marginal budget shares, 29
Marginal cost, 10–11
Marginal revenue, 10–11

Marginal utility, 10
  and consumer demand, 8
  of goods within commodity groups, 29
Market demand, 11–12
Micro level data. *See* Individual consumer
    demand
Mitchell, B. M., 65, 66
Models
  choice of functional form for estimating
    equations, 45; double logarithmic ap-
    proach, 46; translog approach, 48–52;
    variable elasticity approach, 47
  data problems influencing, 52, 162
  equilibrium approach to, 43–44
  reduced-form consumption, 15–23; dynamic,
    67–70, 93, 100–103; fuel share, 71–74,
    103–104; static, 61–66, 96–100, 109
  restrictions imposed by structure of, 53
  structural demand, 23–27, 42–43, 74–77,
    104–105
Moore, Thomas G., 62, 63, 64
Morrison, C. J., 148
Mount, T. D., 68, 82
Mowill, R. S., 65, 66

National Economic Research Associates, Inc.
    (NERA), 85, 89
Natural gas
  disequilibrium in market for, 43–44, 92, 113,
    155
  identification problem and, 106
  industrial demand for: deficiencies in studies
    of, 106–107, 113; by electricity genera-
    tion, 110–113; fuel shares models for,
    105–107; by manufacturing, 105–106,
    107–109; price elasticity of, 105–107, 109,
    111–112, 160; static models for, 109
  price-quantity interdependence for, 35, 39–
    40, 99–100
  residential and commercial demand for:
    compared with electricity demand, 93;
    deficiencies in studies of, 105; dynamic
    consumption models for, 93, 100–103;
    fuel shares models for, 103–104; and gas
    appliances replacement, 100–102; in-
    come elasticity of, 96, 97; price elasticity
    of, 93, 96, 97, 105, 159–160; by regional
    markets, 102–103; static consumption
    models for, 96–100; structural models
    for, 104–105
NERA. *See* National Economic Research Asso-
    ciates, Inc.
Neri, John A., 93, 97
Nerlove, Marc, 69, 72
New York Gas Group, 97
Nuclear power, 137

Olson, Charles E., 93, 97
Organisation for Economic Cooperation and
    Development, estimates of gasoline con-
    sumption by, 119

Pearce, I. F., 30
Petroleum products

  data on consumption of, 32, 114
  disequilibrium in market for, 45
  transportation demand for, 114–116
  see also Diesel fuel; Fuel oil; Gasoline
Phlips, Louis, 122
Pindyck, Robert S., 102
Polynomial lag scheme, 20–21, 67, 83
Pooled samples, 52
  advantages and disadvantages of, 151–152
  explanation of, 20
  to measure electricity demand, 61, 67
  to measure gasoline demand, 118
Price controls, for petroleum products, 45
Price elasticity
  in aggregate demand functions, 29, 31, 33
  coal, 137, 141, 142, 144
  electricity, 56, 60, 62–66, 68–70, 73–79, 83,
    85, 87–91, 158
  explanation of, 13
  factors causing differences in estimates of, 2–3
  fuel oil, 129, 133
  functional forms for, 46–51, 52
  gasoline, 116, 120–123, 125, 126–127, 160
  income and, 1, 8, 46–47, 48, 53, 151
  long-run versus short-run, 17, 23, 147–149;
    for coal, 137, 141, 161; for electricity, 60,
    68, 75–76, 79, 158; for fuel oil, 133, 161;
    for gasoline, 116, 119, 123–125, 160; for
    natural gas, 98, 159
  natural gas, 81, 97, 103, 104, 109
  nongasoline transportation fuels, 127–128
  regional differences in, 111
  see also Cross-price elasticity
Prices, energy
  average, 36, 37–38, 98
  energy equipment, 14–15, 42
  interdependence of quantity and, 35–41
  marginal, 35, 38–39, 98, 99
  multiple schedule for, 36
  separation from other influences on demand,
    52–53
Primary metals industry
  coal demand by, 142, 144
  fuel oil demand by, 131, 133
  natural gas demand by, 109
Producer demand for energy
  market demand function to estimate, 11–12
  output level and input prices effect on 8–10
Profits
  maximization, 47
  restricted, 50
Puig, Carlos, 26, 63, 64, 66, 75

Ramsey, J. B., 118, 119
Rasche, R., 118, 119
Reddy, Nallapu N., 141, 142, 144
Reduced-form consumption models
  deficiencies in, 17, 21–22
  to distinguish between long-run and short-run
    adjustments, 17–18
  dynamic, 18–21; for electricity, 60, 61, 67–70;
    for gasoline, 120–122; for natural gas, 93,
    100–104
  explanation of, 15–16

fuel shares, 16–17; for electricity, 71–74; for fuel oil, 131; for natural gas, 103–104
lag-adjustment, 18–20
static, 17–18; for electricity, 60, 61–66; for gasoline, 118–120; for natural gas, 96–100
Regulations
  coal demand and environmental, 136–138
  and electricity prices, 63
  and market equilibrium, 34, 43–44
Resek, Robert W., 124
Residential sector
  aggregation of fuel consumption in, 28, 30, 31
  data on electricity consumption in, 31, 32
  electricity demand by, 55–79
  energy demand studies for, 152
  fuel oil demand by, 128–129, 131
  interdependence of fuel prices and quantities for, 40–41
  measurement of fuel consumption in, 16
  natural gas demand by, 93–105
Robeson, Franklin E., 93, 97
Rodekohr, Mark, 26, 116, 124

Schultz, Henry, 33
Sheehan, Dennis, 120, 121
Spann, Robert, 73, 104
Springer, Robert K., 124
Standard Industrial Classification, 32
Stanford Research Institute, 75
Strotz, Robert H., 29
Structural demand models
  deficiencies in, 24, 25
  differentiation of short-run and long-run behavior by, 147, 149
  explanation of, 23–24
  for gasoline demand, 123–125
  reduced-form models compared with, 27
  for residential and commercial natural gas demand, 104–105
  for residential electricity demand, 74–77
Substitution
  elasticity of interfuel, 2, 46, 49; coal, 137, 139; electricity, 71-74; in electricity generation, 109–113; fuel oil, 129, 131, 133, 134; functional form for, 46, 48; natural gas, 107; in reduced-form models, 15–18, 71–74

factor, 48, 50–51
Sweeney, James, 26, 116, 124

Taylor, Lester D., 19, 25, 35, 36, 67, 75, 103, 129
TEBs. See Typical electrical bills
Technology
  and demand for coal, 135–136
  and industrial demand for electricity, 91
  and input-output combinations, 9
Time series data
  for electricity demand, 61, 67, 90
  for gasoline consumption, 118
  for natural gas demand, 108–109
  for short-term adjustments, 17, 147
Translog model, 48–52, 156
  for natural gas demand, 109, 110, 112
Transportation
  demand for gasoline, 116–127
  demand for nongasoline fuels, 127–128
  demand for petroleum products, 114–116
  disaggregation of fuel consumption in, 30–31
Typical electrical bills (TEBs)
  to measure commercial consumption, 81–82
  to measure residential consumption, 38, 39, 63, 64, 73, 76
Tyrrell, T. J., 68, 82

Unit cost function, 23, 49–50
  for electricity, 89
  for fuel oil, 133
  translog approximation for natural gas, 109
Uri, Noel D., 67, 82, 83, 110, 133, 140
Utility function, 47, 122
Utility maximization, 35, 47

Verleger, Philip K., Jr., 25, 36, 75, 103, 120, 121, 129

Washington Center for Metropolitan Studies, 66, 96
Watkins, G. C., 102, 103, 148
Waverman, Leonard, 49
Weierstrass theorem, 20
Wills, J., 65
Wilson, John W., 62, 89
Wood, David O., 89

Zerhoot, Frederick, 17, 83, 107, 131, 142